AF478008

Por Convención Ferrer

The North West, Anarcho-Syndicalism & Time Travel

First published 2008 by
Liverpool University Press
4 Cambridge Street
Liverpool L69 7ZU

Copyright © 2008 David Jacques
The author's rights have been asserted by him in accordance with the Copyright, Designs and Patents Act 1988.

All rights reserved. No part of this book may be reproduced, stored in a retrieval system, or transmitted, in any form or by any means, electronic, mechanical, photocopying, recording, or otherwise, without the prior written permission of the publisher.

British Library Cataloguing-in-Publication data
A British Library CIP record is available

ISBN 978-1-84631-206-9
Designed by March Graphic Design Studio, Liverpool
Printed and bound by Gutenberg Press, Malta

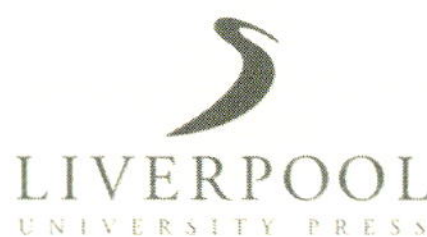

Por Convención Ferrer

The North West, Anarcho-Syndicalism & Time Travel

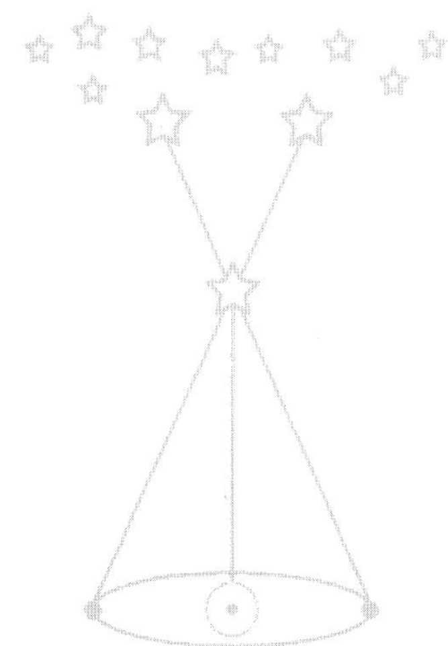

David Jacques

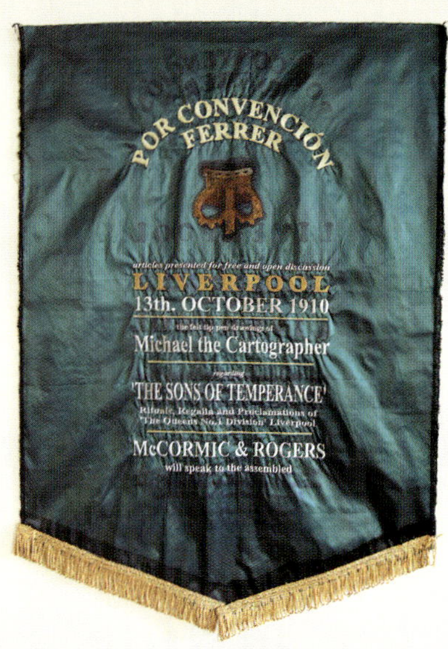
POR CONVENCIÓN FERRER
articles presented for free and open discussion
LIVERPOOL
13th. OCTOBER 1910
Michael the Cartographer
'THE SONS OF TEMPERANCE'
McCORMIC & ROGERS
will speak to the assembled

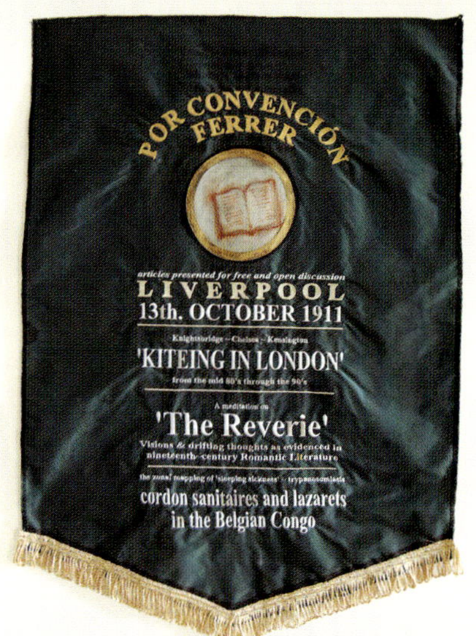
POR CONVENCIÓN FERRER
articles presented for free and open discussion
LIVERPOOL
13th. OCTOBER 1911
Knightsbridge – Chelsea – Kensington
'KITEING IN LONDON'
from the mid 80's through the 90's
A meditation on
'The Reverie'
Visions & drifting thoughts as evidenced in nineteenth-century Romantic Literature
cordon sanitaires and lazarets in the Belgian Congo

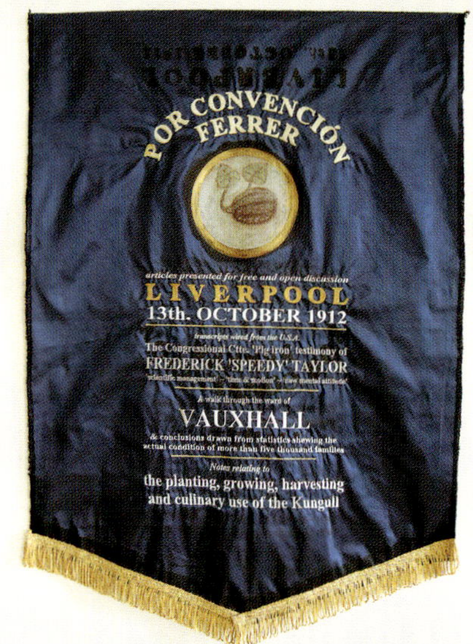
POR CONVENCIÓN FERRER
articles presented for free and open discussion
LIVERPOOL
13th. OCTOBER 1912
FREDERICK 'SPEEDY' TAYLOR
VAUXHALL
the planting, growing, harvesting and culinary use of the Kungull

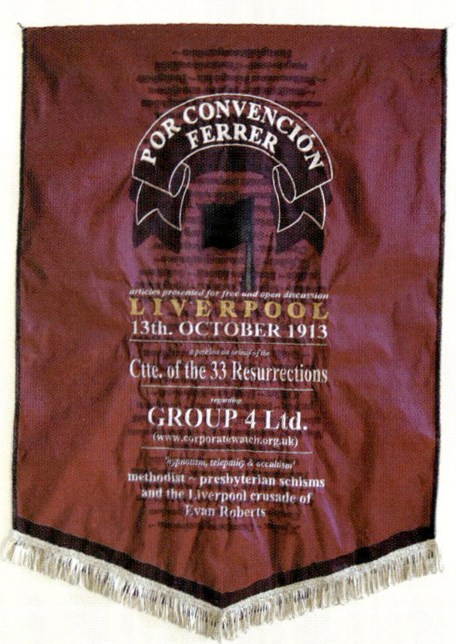
POR CONVENCIÓN FERRER
articles presented for free and open discussion
LIVERPOOL
13th. OCTOBER 1913
Ctte. of the 33 Resurrections
GROUP 4 Ltd.
(www.corporatewatch.org.uk)
methodist – presbyterian schisms and the Liverpool crusade of Evan Roberts

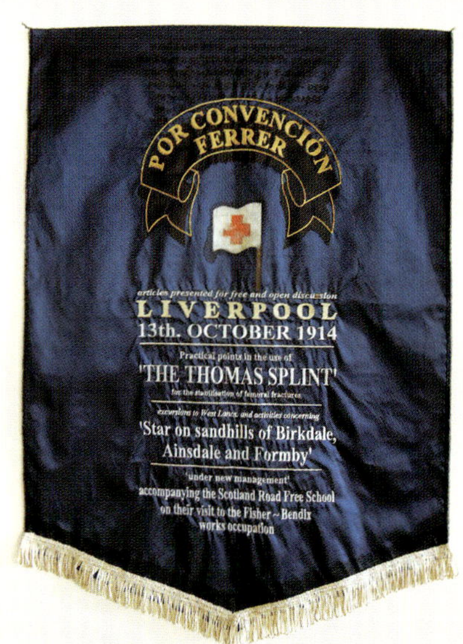
POR CONVENCIÓN FERRER
articles presented for free and open discussion
LIVERPOOL
13th. OCTOBER 1914
Practical points in the use of
'THE THOMAS SPLINT'
'Star on sandhills of Birkdale, Ainsdale and Formby'
'under new management'
accompanying the Scotland Road Free School on their visit to the Fisher – Bendix works occupation

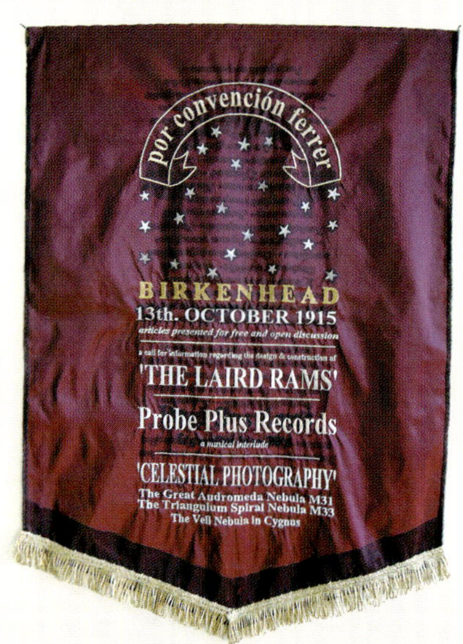
por convención ferrer
BIRKENHEAD
13th. OCTOBER 1915
articles presented for free and open discussion
'THE LAIRD RAMS'
Probe Plus Records
a musical interlude
'CELESTIAL PHOTOGRAPHY'
The Great Andromeda Nebula M31
The Triangulum Spiral Nebula M33
The Veil Nebula in Cygnus

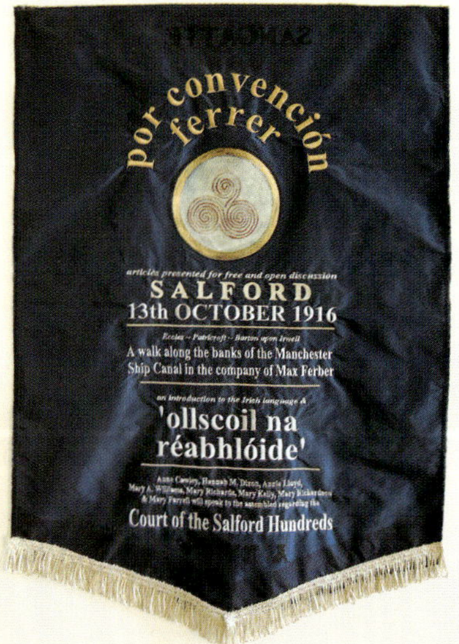
por convención ferrer
articles presented for free and open discussion
SALFORD
13th OCTOBER 1916
A walk along the banks of the Manchester Ship Canal in the company of Max Ferber
'ollscoil na réabhlóide'
Court of the Salford Hundreds

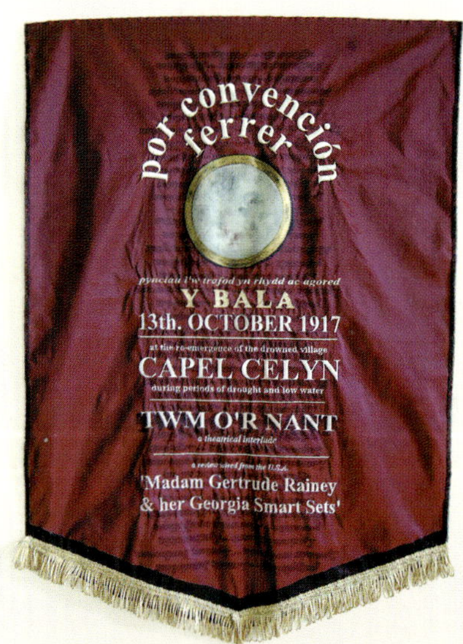
por convención ferrer
Y BALA
13th. OCTOBER 1917
CAPEL CELYN
during periods of drought and low water
TWM O'R NANT
a theatrical interlude
'Madam Gertrude Rainey & her Georgia Smart Sets'

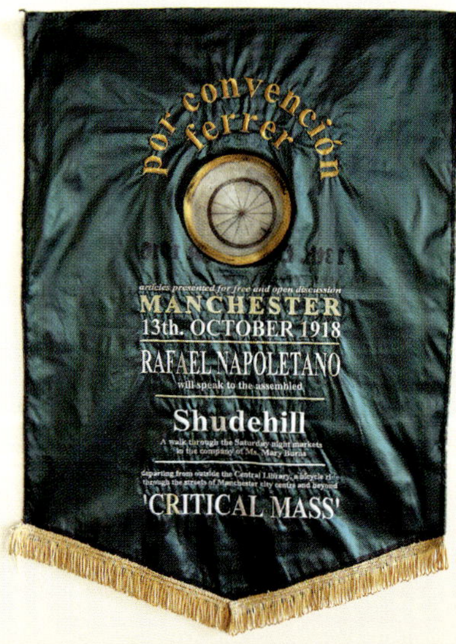
por convención ferrer
articles presented for free and open discussion
MANCHESTER
13th. OCTOBER 1918
RAFAEL NAPOLETANO
will speak to the assembled
Shudehill
'CRITICAL MASS'

Por Convención Ferrer
1910–1918

In the years leading up to the First World War a small though significant network of Anarchist (specifically Anarcho-syndicalist) activists made their presence felt in downtown Liverpool. The Syndicalist advocacy of 'direct action' to influence industrial disputes found plenty of scope for activity around the city, particularly in the Docklands.

At the same time, an element within the group was concentrating its efforts on developing new and distinct programmes of education.[1] One event, an annual conference-cum-discussion group, emerged under the title 'Por Convención Ferrer'.

From 1910, held on 13 October each year and named in honour of the Spanish educationalist Francisco Ferrer y Guardia,[2] Por Convención Ferrer provided a platform for anyone to propose *'... for free and open discussion'* any subject of their choosing. The contributions generally came from anonymous sources or from within the group itself, they were broad ranging in their subject matter and had often been realised by undertaking some form of time travel.

The events ran until 1918, and along the way some took place at other venues, supported by sympathetic parties in Birkenhead, Bala, Salford and Manchester.

[1] See Bob Holton, 'Syndicalism and Labour in Merseyside 1906–14', in *Building the Union* (Toulouse Press, 1973): 'Anarcho-syndicalists on Merseyside as elsewhere were not purely concerned with industrial problems. Their revolutionary commitment involved other forms of activity, suited to the establishment of an alternative society based on an alternative social morality. To this end particular attention was devoted to independent educational organisations [...] The influence of Spanish political refugees was especially important in this work. Lorenzo Portet, who had settled in Liverpool in 1907, was a close friend of Francisco Ferrer, the leading Anarchist educational reformer in Spain. Ferrer's "Modern Schools" were intended to challenge the clerical stranglehold on education in that country, in favour of a secular and rational approach to learning. Ferrer visited Liverpool on at least two occasions between 1907–09, encouraging others to establish similar educational organisations on Merseyside.'

[2] Ferrer was tried and executed on 13 October 1909 for his alleged involvement with a violent uprising in Barcelona.

Notes

Archive. 'Por Convención Ferrer' begins with a concocted archive, a series of commemorative pennants, inscribed with the titles presented at each conference. On close inspection, the painted-embroidered silks are fairly rough in their construction, with off-centred pattern registrations, colour bleeds and barely decipherable texts staining a palimpsest-like surface. They figure more as a series of templates, remnants from a studio or 'works in progress'. Possibly produced at a point of negotiation – prior to confirmation of the proposed events.

Text / Narrative. The text has been gathered together from a broad spectrum of sources and presented by a researcher / narrator, who gives way to a variety of voices – either the subjects themselves or commentaries contemporaneous to the subject. Twenty-seven narratives emerge at varying stages of 'trajectory', or realisation. Each story presents a change of step in register, ranging from the everyday to the catastrophic. No linkage is offered and the seemingly haphazard juxtaposition of events renders a fractured, disconnected voyage through time, space and place.

The presentations take on a range of forms (discussions, field trips, performances etc.) and media (websites, newspapers, telegraphs etc.). Contributions are also drawn from fictitious characters, spectral appearances, hallucinatory / dream-like transcendences to places located either in the past or the future (on occasion there is a suggestion that the group may even have left their mark; see 'Star on Sandhills', 'The Laird Rams').

Time-shift. The nine gatherings staged between 1910 and 1918 each entail three presentations. Each presentation references a point in time; one takes on a point approximately concurrent with each conference (1910–18), a second sees a point fifty years or more into the past, and a third undertakes a point fifty years or more into the future. The first ('Michael the Cartographer') and the final ('Critical Mass') contributions could, through the posited figure of a *parallax*, present as *spatial vantage points* from where the intervening 'constellation' of issues can be viewed.

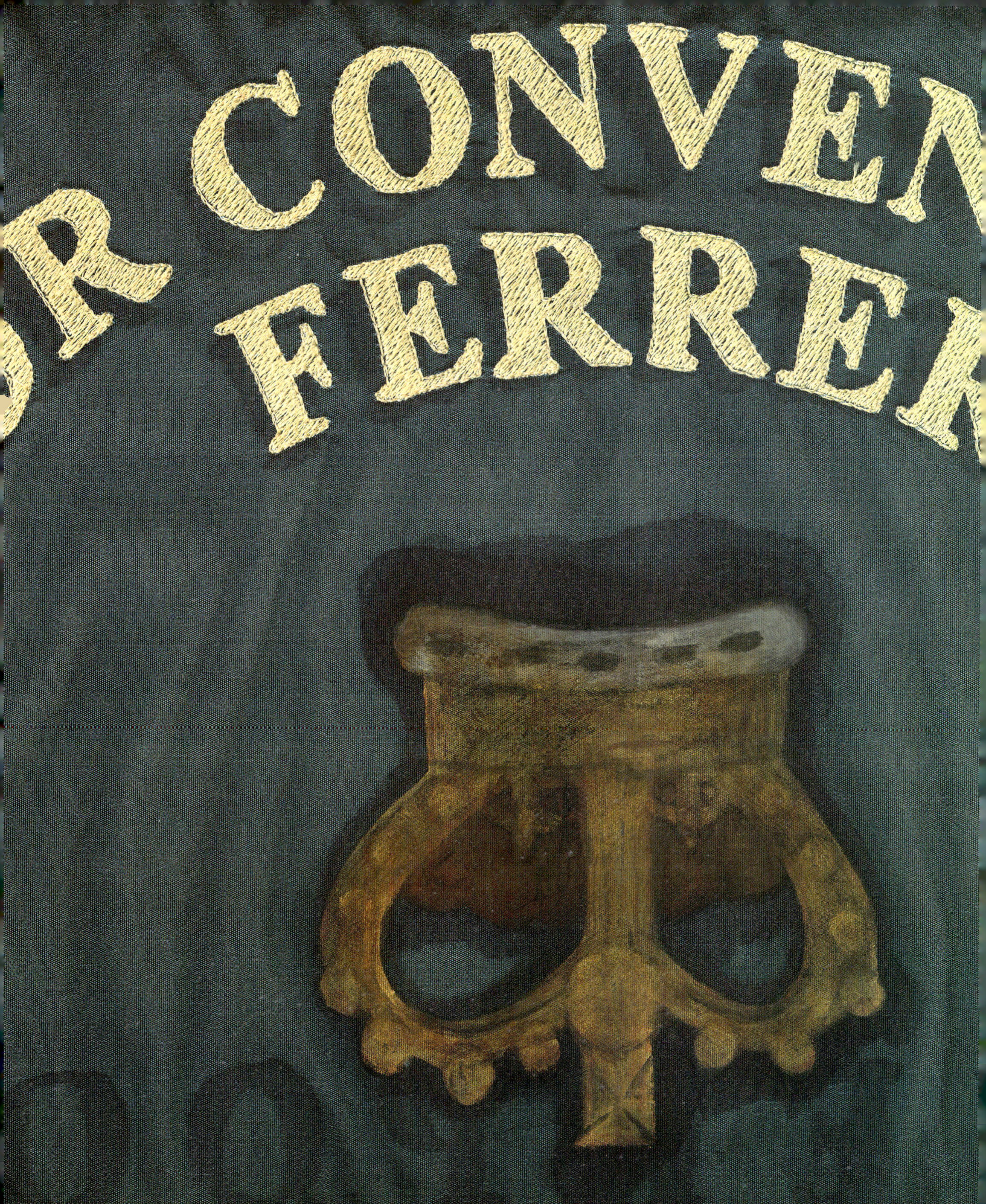
R CONVEN
FERRE

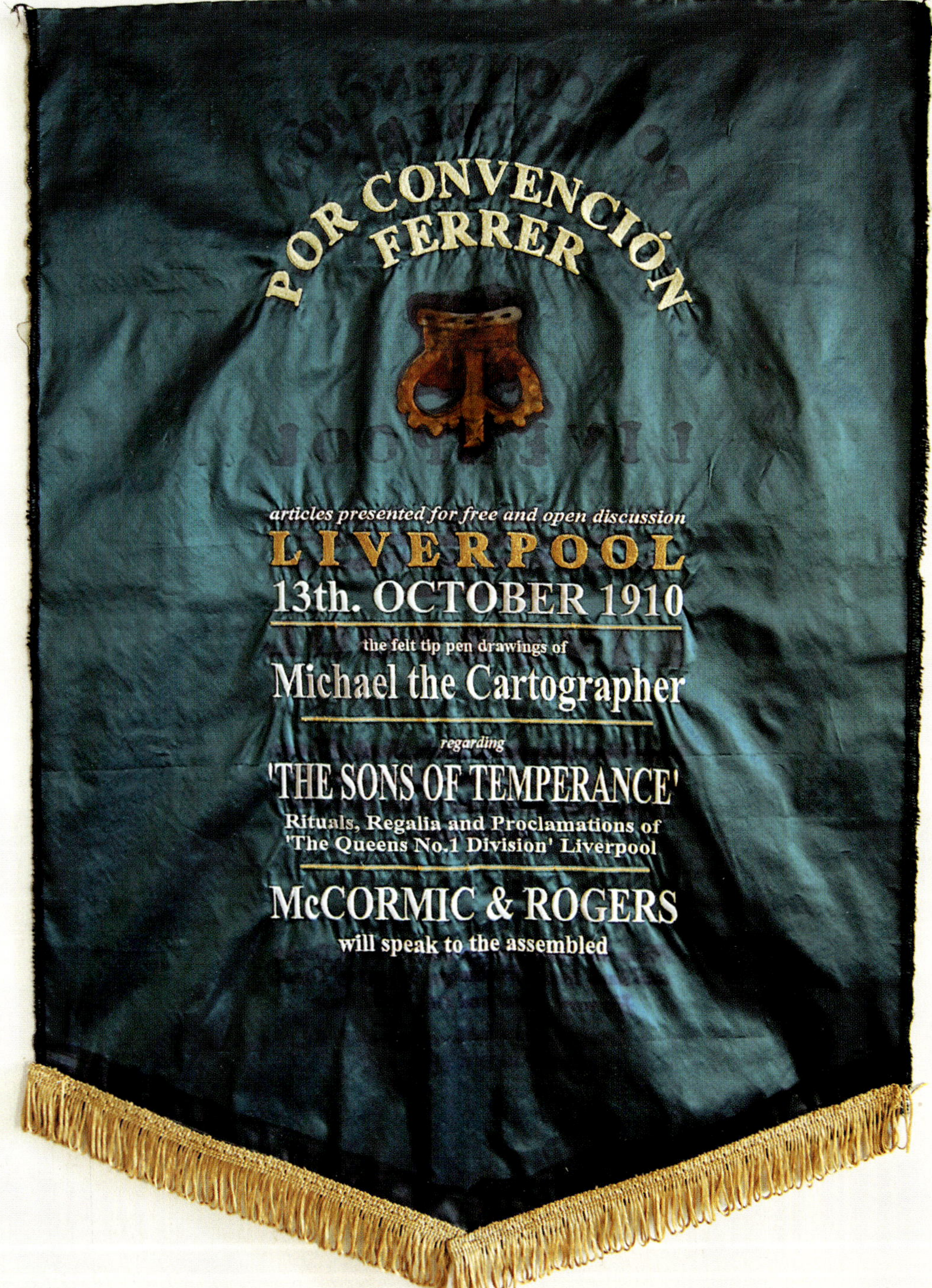

POR CONVENCIÓN
FERRER
articles presented for free and open discussion
LIVERPOOL
13th. OCTOBER 1910
the felt tip pen drawings of
Michael the Cartographer
regarding
'THE SONS OF TEMPERANCE'
Rituals, Regalia and Proclamations of
'The Queens No.1 Division' Liverpool
McCORMIC & ROGERS
will speak to the assembled

The first meeting entailed the viewing and discussion of a small exhibition, a debate examining the make-up of a prominent 'benevolent' organisation and a speech delivered by two young local men.

Por Convención Ferrer

LIVERPOOL

13 October 1910

the felt-tip pen drawings of
Michael the Cartographer

regarding
'The Sons of Temperance'
Rituals, Regalia and Proclamations of
'The Queens 1st. Division' Liverpool

McCormic & Rogers
will speak to the assembled

Michael the Cartographer approached the collector Victor Musgrave sometime in the early 1980s. He gave no information about his background or any possible relationship to the artworld. It seems that he lived in isolation and spent long periods of time making detailed maps of non-existent places most of which he reputedly destroyed.

'The Sons of Temperance' originated in the United States and established their first English Division in Liverpool. 1910 would see in their 60th year of operations. Widely regarded as a Masonic-like organisation, the movement often took the form of a religious revival and was referred to as a crusade. Drink became 'the demon', the pledge echoed baptism, and the solemn reading of the names of backsliders was a form of excommunication.

'The Sons of Temperance took the lead in England in demonstrating the propriety and practicability of both men and women mingling in secret society lodges … evidenced by its mode of initiation, the form of the obligation and the manner of religious worship.' Albert C. Stevens, *The Cyclopaedia of Fraternities*, New York, Hamilton Printing and Publishing Co., 1899

McCormic and Rogers will speak to the assembled. McCormic and Rogers were both executed at Lancaster on 22 April 1820. From a handbill entitled 'The Last Dying Speech': *'Phillip Rogers aged 23 and Peter McCormic 26, for selling Bank of England notes at a less price than their nominal value in Liverpool. According to the evidence on the trial of McCormic, it appears that the unhappy man, sold one week with another, at least one thousand forged notes. The Judge in passing sentence on these unfortunate men most solemnly admonished them to prepare for the speedy death which awaited them. His Lordship observed that the extensive manner in which they had disseminated this pernicious traffic rendered it inconsistent with his duty to hold out to them the least shadow of mercy. Since their conviction, their behaviour has been in every degree such as might have been expected in their awful situation, they acknowledged the justness of his sentence, and they profess they shall die in peace with all men, in hopes of a speedy and joyful resurrection.'*

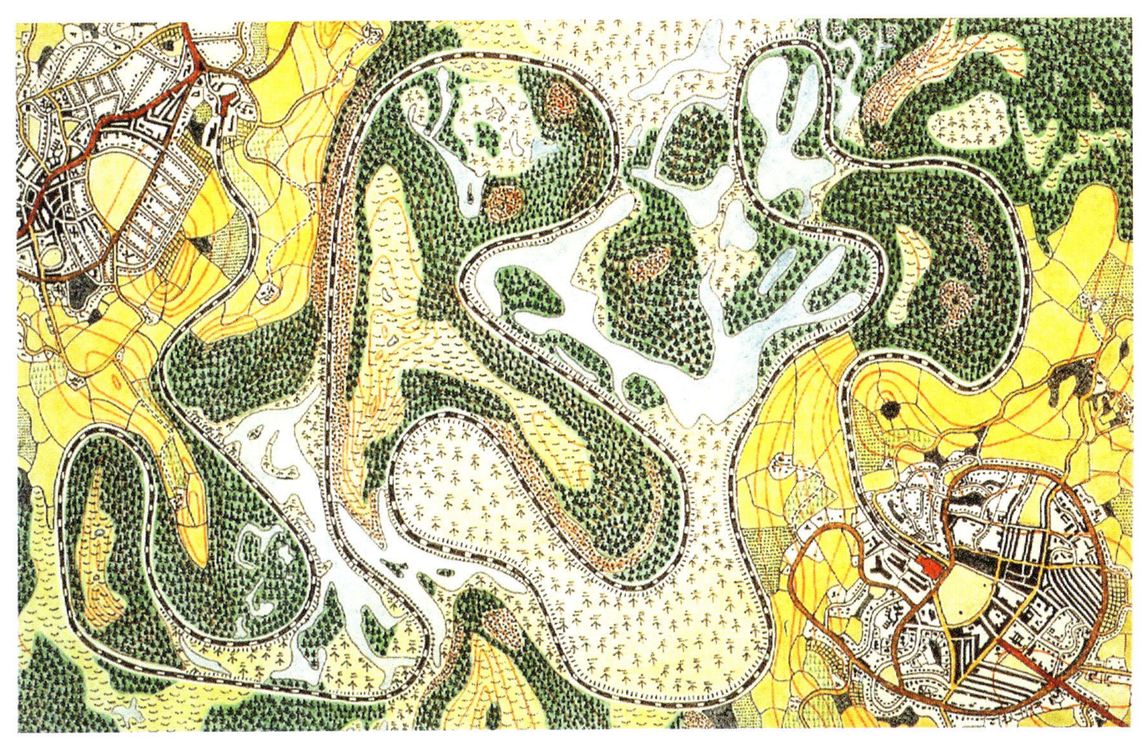

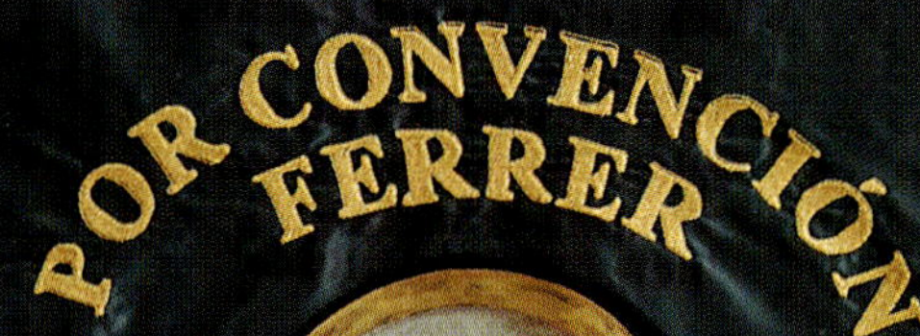

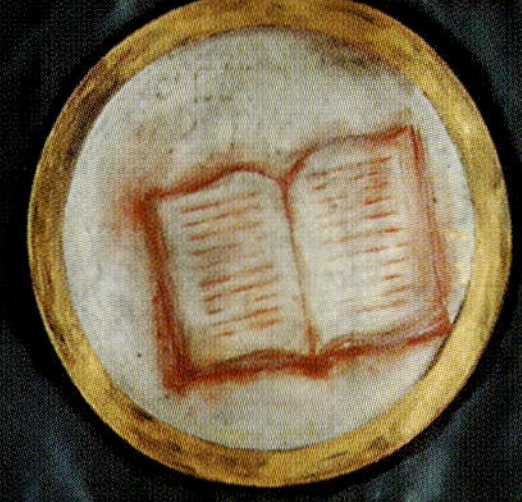

articles presented for free and open discussion

LIVERPOOL

13th. OCTOBER 1911

Knightsbridge ~ Chelsea ~ Kensington

'KITEING IN LONDON'

from the mid 80's through the 90's

A meditation on

'The Reverie'

Visions & drifting thoughts as evidenced in
nineteenth~century Romantic Literature

the zonal mapping of 'sleeping sickness' ~ trypanosomiasis

cordon sanitaires and lazarets
in the Belgian Congo

The second gathering involved a conversation regarding the practice of ‘kiteing’, an ‘appearance’ by the author Thomas De Quincey and a report on the Belgian Congo sleeping sickness epidemic.

Por Convención Ferrer

LIVERPOOL

13 October 1911

Knightsbridge – Chelsea – Kensington
‘Kiteing in London’
from the mid-80s through the 90s

A meditation on
‘The Reverie’
Visions and drifting thoughts as evidenced in
nineteenth-century Romantic Literature

The zonal mapping of ‘sleeping sickness’ – trypanosomiasis
cordon sanitaires and lazarets in
the Belgian Congo

Knightsbridge – Chelsea – Kensington. 'Kiteing in London'. From the mid-80s through the 90s. 'Kiteing' is a slang term for the use of a chequebook / credit card reported as lost or stolen. The favoured purchases tended to be expensive items of clothing from exclusive designer stores. These would invariably be sold on to secure a cash return. Information gleaned from a phone call made between the speaker and an 'acquaintance' related the ups and downs of 'kiteing' around a selection of London's up-market boroughs.

A meditation on 'The Reverie'. Visions and drifting thoughts as evidenced in nineteenth-century Romantic Literature.
'I often fell into these reveries upon taking opium; and more than once it happened to me, on a summer night, when I have been at an open window, in a room from which I could overlook the sea at a mile below me, and could command a view of the great town of L_, at about the same distance, that I have sate from sun-set to sun-rise, motionless, and without wishing to move. I shall be charged with mysticism, Behmenism, quietism, &c, but that shall not alarm me ... [T]he scene itself was somewhat typical of what took place in such a reverie. The town of L_ represented the earth, with it's sorrows and it's graves left behind, yet not out of sight, nor wholly forgotten. The ocean, in everlasting but gentle agitation, and brooded over by a dove-like calm, might not unfitly typify the mind and the mood which then swayed it. For it seemed to me as if then first I stood at a distance, and aloof from the uproar of life as if the tumult, the fever, and the strife, were suspended; a respite granted from the secret burthens of the heart; a Sabbath of repose; a resting from human labours. Here were the hopes which blossom in the paths of life, reconciled with the peace which is in the grave; motions of the intellect as unwearied as the heavens, yet for all anxieties a halcyon calm; a tranquillity that seemed no product of inertia, but as if resulting from mighty and equal antagonisms; infinite activities, infinite repose.' Thomas De Quincey, *Confessions of an English Opium-Eater* (pub. *The London Magazine*, 1821)

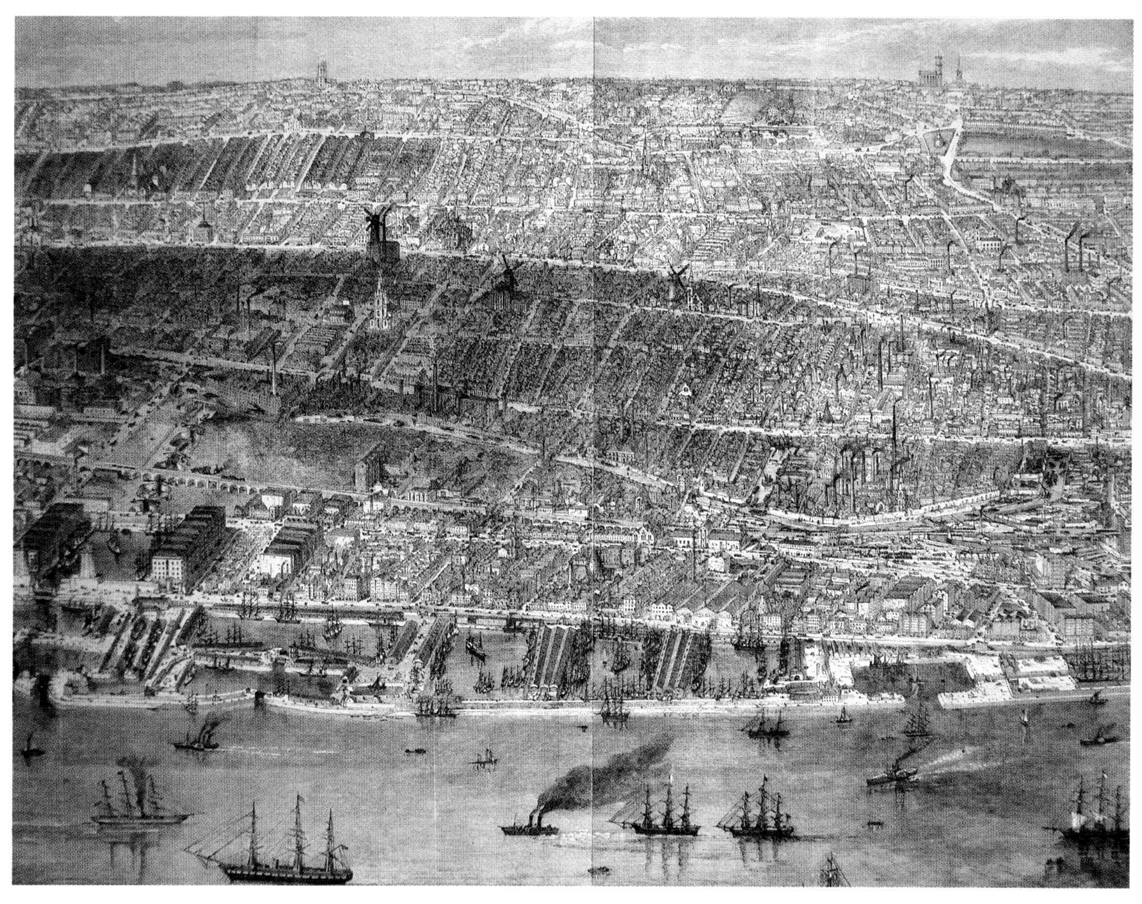

The zonal mapping of 'sleeping sickness' – trypanosomiasis. Cordon sanitaires and lazarets in the Belgian Congo. A research trip undertaken by the Liverpool School of Tropical Medicine in 1904 at the behest of King Leopold II, declared sleeping sickness to be epidemic in parts of the Congo Free State (the disease had already claimed 250,000 lives in Uganda and was spreading through other African colonies). Their advice was to impose an immediate set of controls to stem the further spread of the outbreak. In attempting to contain the disease, the Belgian Authorities imposed a restriction of movement on people living in infected areas. Many were confined to a cordon sanitaire, or were limited in their passage from zone to zone by checkpoints and the possession of a medical passport.

Leopold's commissioning of the Liverpool School to investigate the epidemic in reality betokened a need to enhance his international image. The Congo Free State was effectively a private empire brutally and exploitatively controlled by Leopold alone; it attracted condemnation from humanitarian groups who campaigned vociferously to expose the activities of his regime (notably the collected letters and speeches of the Congo Reform Association, founded by E.D. Morel, Dr Henry Guinness and Roger Casement, published in 1911). By acting in a seemingly benevolent way Leopold thought he might stabilise the condition of his labour force, while at the same time be seen to actively support a prestigious international quest.

'After we'd finished telling the old man how to make the Congo healthy and promised to administer a lovely coat of whitewash to his character in the eyes of the English, he created Boyce, Ross and myself officers of his Order of Leopold II … We commenced yesterday what is intended to become quite a political move – an entente cordiale – a renewal of the intimacy of Belgium and England …' Dr J.L. Todd, Letters (23 August 1906), Liverpool School of Tropical Medicine Archives

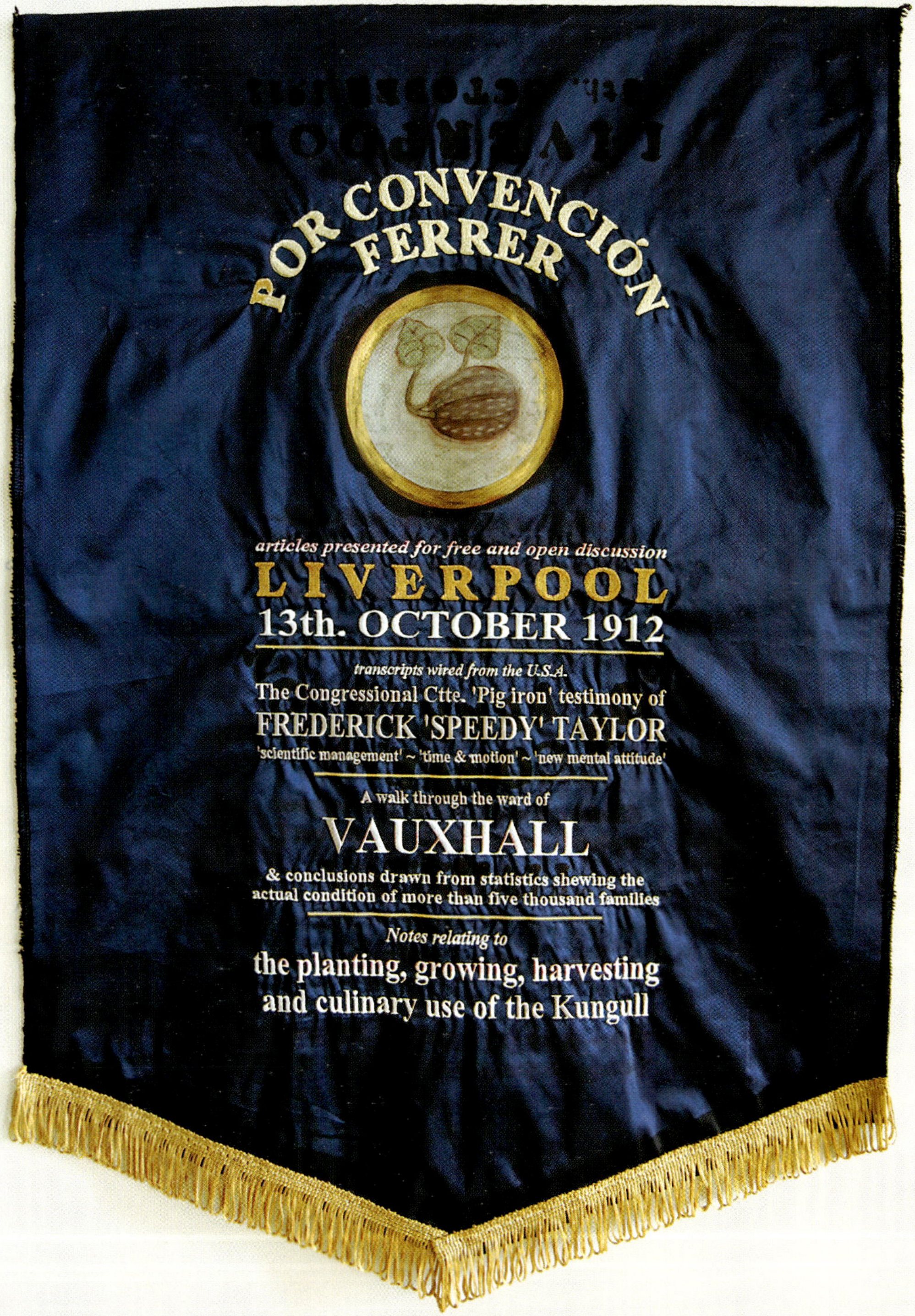

POR CONVENCIÓN
FERRER

articles presented for free and open discussion

LIVERPOOL

13th. OCTOBER 1912

transcripts wired from the U.S.A.

The Congressional Ctte. 'Pig iron' testimony of

FREDERICK 'SPEEDY' TAYLOR

'scientific management' ~ 'time & motion' ~ 'new mental attitude'

A walk through the ward of

VAUXHALL

& conclusions drawn from statistics shewing the
actual condition of more than five thousand families

Notes relating to

the planting, growing, harvesting
and culinary use of the Kungull

The 1912 meeting saw a reading from a transcription of a Congressional Committee session in the USA, a walk through the Vauxhall ward of 1842 (investigating at first hand aspects of a study conducted by John Finch Jr), and a discussion on the 'Kungull', a type of pumpkin common to Balkan regions that was being grown on a Liverpool allotment.

Por Convención Ferrer

LIVERPOOL

13 October 1912

Transcripts wired from the U.S.A.
The Congressional Ctte. 'Pig Iron' testimony of
Frederick 'Speedy' Taylor
'scientific management' – 'time & motion' – 'new mental attitude'

a walk through the ward of
Vauxhall
& 'conclusions drawn from statistics shewing the
actual condition of more than five thousand families'

notes relating to
the planting, growing, harvesting
and culinary use of the Kungull

Transcripts wired from the USA. The Congressional Ctte. 'Pig Iron' testimony of Frederick 'Speedy' Taylor. 'Scientific management' – 'time & motion' – 'new mental attitude'.

Frederick 'Speedy' Taylor, the acknowledged 'father of business efficiency' had a reputation for eccentricity. As a child he insisted when he played with friends that their games conform to rigid rules. Later in life he determined that the longer he slept the shorter he would live; to this end he had invented a device that woke him if he dozed off in his chair.

Taylor was convinced the theories he advocated, to which he applied the term 'Scientific Management', would provide the solution to all social ills. His adage '*regularity and order lead to prosperity and efficiency*' was played out through the application of the stopwatch to the shop floor, calculating detailed timings of physical movements and planning 'round the clock' regimented work schedules. His ideas, universally adopted by early 20th-century industrialists, would find their way most notoriously into the assembly line practice of Henry Ford's car plants. His schemes met with considerable opposition and eventually in 1912 a Congressional Committee was set up to investigate his methods:

CHAIRMAN: *Then, how does scientific management propose to take care of men who are not 'first class' men in any particular line of work?*

TAYLOR: I give up.

CHAIRMAN: *Scientific management has no place for such men?*

TAYLOR: Scientific management has no place for a bird that can sing and won't sing.

CHAIRMAN: *I am not speaking about birds at all.*

TAYLOR: No man who can work and won't work has any place under scientific management.

CHAIRMAN: *It is not a question of a man who can work and won't work, it is a question of a man who is not a 'first class' man in any one particular line, according to your own definition.*

TAYLOR: I do not know of any such line of work. For each man some line can be found in which he is first class. There is work for each type of man, just as for instance, work for the dray horse and work for the trotting horse, and each of these is 'first class' in his particular kind of work. There is no type of work, however, that suits all types of men.

CHAIRMAN: *We are not in this particular investigation dealing with horses nor singing birds … what I wanted to get at is whether or not your scientific management had any place whatever for a man who was not able to meet your own definition of what constitutes a 'first class' workman.*

TAYLOR: Exactly, there is no place for a man who can work and won't work.

CHAIRMAN: *It is not a question of a man who can work and won't work, it is a question of a man who doesn't meet your definition of 'first class' workmen. What place have you for such men?*

TAYLOR: I believe the only man who does not come under 'first class' as I have defined it, is the man who can work and won't work. I have tried to make it clear that for each type of workman some types of work can be found at which he is 'first class', with the exception of those men who are perfectly well able to do the job but won't do it.

A walk through the ward of Vauxhall & conclusions drawn from statistics shewing the actual condition of more than five thousand families. In 1842 the Liverpool Anti-Monopoly Association published a set of statistics compiled by John Finch Jr concerning employment, health, standards of housing etc. in the Vauxhall ward. According to the preface, the figures '*at once convinced the most sceptical, that a degree of wretchedness existed which it was no longer safe to conceal*' ('Statistics of Vauxhall Ward, Liverpool', Liverpool Anti-Monopoly Association, pub. J. Walmsley, London, 1842). Finch, who came from a family renowned for their radical beliefs, also presented a series of 'conclusions' from his findings, which the Association (generally comprising of local small business owners whose trade had slumped) chose to omit from the final publication.

Notes relating to the planting, growing, harvesting and culinary use of the Kungull. The notes referred to were written in the autumn of 2004 by a refugee from Kosova who is involved with the Family Refugee Support Project. The project '*aims to improve and increase the understanding of the mental health needs of refugees and asylum seeker families in Liverpool. Supporting family functioning, increasing independence and social networks and peer support through the use of horticulture.*' The Kungull is a type of pumpkin native to the Balkans and is a popular and valued foodstuff among the Kosovan community. It was introduced to the project's Liverpool allotment through a small number of seeds brought over from Kosova and has produced a successful crop every year.

Ky është një Kungull
i mbjellë në Maj
të këtij viti fara
është sjellë në
Angli nga Kosova
nga një person
që është në vizitë
atje, daja i
babait tim.

Kjo është një
lule e kungullit
ka ngjyre te
verdhe dhe aromatike
dhe është e qëndrue-
shme rreth dy javë
dhe mbyllet. dhe
rritet sa një
shuplakë dore

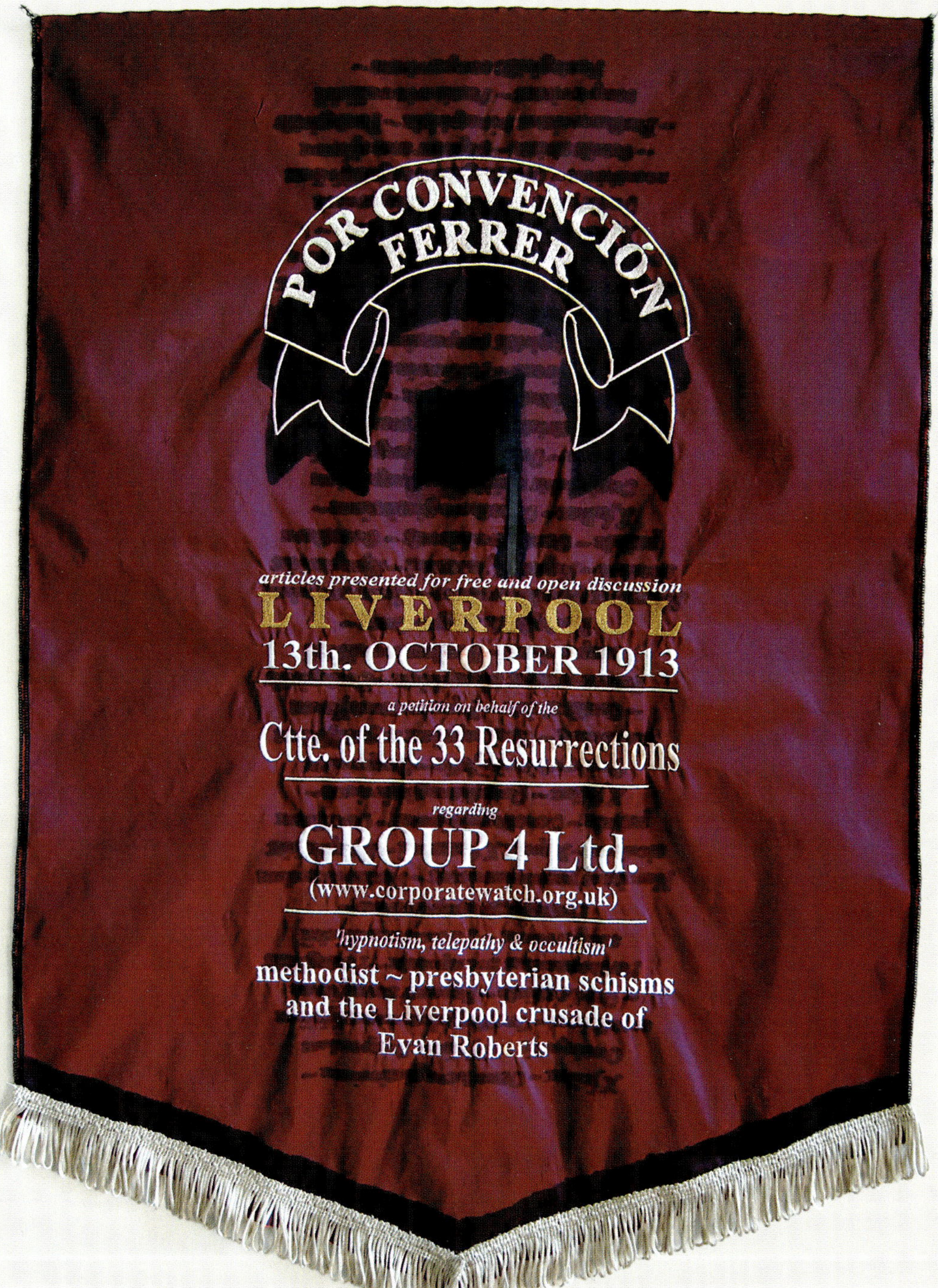
POR CONVENCIÓN
FERRER
articles presented for free and open discussion
LIVERPOOL
13th. OCTOBER 1913
a petition on behalf of the
Ctte. of the 33 Resurrections
regarding
GROUP 4 Ltd.
(www.corporatewatch.org.uk)
'hypnotism, telepathy & occultism'
methodist ~ presbyterian schisms
and the Liverpool crusade of
Evan Roberts

The conference of 1913 commenced with the reading of a petition, a viewing of the 'Corporatewatch' website and an assessment of the Revivalist preacher Evan Roberts' activities in Liverpool.

Por Convención Ferrer

LIVERPOOL

13 October 1913

A petition on behalf of the
Ctte. of the 33 Resurrections

Regarding
Group 4 Ltd.
(www.corporatewatch.org.uk)

'hypnotism, telepathy & occultism'
Methodist–Presbyterian schisms and the Liverpool crusade of Evan Roberts

A petition on behalf of the Ctte. of the 33 Resurrections.

'WHOLESALE RESURRECTIONISTS – Instances of the disinterment of one or two human bodies, for the purpose of dissection, have occasionally come within our knowledge, in this town, as well as others; but it would seem, that a discovery made on Tuesday, that there has existed, an organised company of resurrectionists in Liverpool, for the purpose of supplying the medical students of Edinburgh with subjects for dissection on a large scale. The following is an account of the circumstances connected with this extraordinary affair, which is altogether unparalleled in this town, and has, of course, produced a strong excitement of feeling, and unpleasant sensation amongst all classes of the community. It appears that on Monday afternoon three casks were sent to be shipped on board the Latona *smack, Captain Walker, which was taking in goods for Leith, in Georges Dock Passage. They had been Newfoundland oil casks, and were marked on the outside "Bitter Salts", and accompanied by a shipping note, of which the following is a copy:*

"Please ship on board the Latona *three casks of Bitter Salts, from Mr Brown, agent, Liverpool, to Mr G.H. Ironson Edinburgh.*

Liverpool Oct 9 1826, To the Carron Company".

The casks were put down between decks, to be stowed away in their proper place the following morning. Before this was accomplished, the men employed in moving them were much annoyed by an offensive smell which proceeded from the casks, and informed the Captain of this circumstance. Upon a closer examination, the Captain found a small hole in one of the casks stopped up with a whisp of hay, and, upon drawing it out, the stench became almost intolerable. He then started one of the bungs, and, upon putting his hand in the hole, found, to his utter surprise, that the contents of the casks were human bodies. Assured of this fact, he hastened to communicate the same to his owners, the Carron Company, in Redcross Street. The respectable agent of that establishment promptly apprized the Police of the discovery, who had the casks immediately conveyed to the dead-house, in Chapel Street, where the contents were examined, and found to consist of eleven human bodies, plentifully bestowed with, and packed in salt.

The carter, who had been employed to bring down the casks for shipment in the Latona, *having stated where he brought them from, a party of the Police were sent to examine, and bring away the remaining contents of the cellar in Hope Street. Upon their arrival, they found several casks and sacks full of dead bodies, which were brought down to the dead-house, and underwent an examination by Mr Davis, surgeon, and their contents found to amount (together with the contents of the three casks taken from the vessel) to the extraordinary number of thirty three bodies, of both sexes, and of various ages. They were doubtless intended for dissection at Edinbugh. The person under whose premises this wholesale charnel-house, had unfortunately, been formed, is a gentleman of respectability and character, and will, doubtless, be able to clear himself from any imputation of connivance in the business. It would appear that the disgraceful traffic had been carried on for a considerable time, but by whom, remains to be ascertained; and we fear that the publicity that has already been given to this affair will greatly contribute to the efforts which are now making to bring the delinquents to justice. There does not, at present appear to be any evidence tending to prove whence the bodies were disinterred, and as this subject may hereafter form matter of legal investigation, and, in the absence of positive facts, we shall abstain from giving currency to mere rumour.'*

The Liverpool Mercury, Friday 13 October, 1826

Regarding Group 4 Ltd. A brief time-line relating to Group 4, March '90 to March '98, obtained from the corporatewatch website:

March '90. Norman Fowler joins G4 Securitas Ltd as non-executive director.

April '92. Opening of Wolds prison, Humberside, for remand prisoners. G4 wins £6m management contract.

June '92. Major disturbance at Wolds prison, lasts 7 hours and causes £5,000 damage.

October '92. G4 acquires 50% share-holding in Ecover, the Belgian detergent manufacturer.

April '93. G4 guards fail to prevent Channel Four's chickens being eaten by a fox.

May '93. G4 hires PR company Shandwick Consultants, to deal with the national media. Shandwick is run by Peter Gummer (brother of John), and also does PR for Conservative Party. Drunk prisoner Ernest Hogg chokes on his own vomit whilst in the care of G4 Court Services. Hogg lay unconscious and unnoticed in the back of a prison van for several hours before he died. Six G4 staff have their operating certificates suspended by Home Office. G4 later found guilty of 'lack of care'.

June '93. Barrie Gane, ex-deputy head of MI6, joins G4. A G4 spokesperson says; 'His knowledge of international affairs is particularly useful in the development of our strategy and international growth'. The Green Party calls for a consumer boycott of Ecover products in response to alleged 'brutal aggression' against protesters at Twyford Down.

August '93. Home Office inquiry criticises G4 for using excessive restraint in handling a prisoner. Despite her asthma and low security risk status she was handcuffed and locked in a van cell for two hours. Judge Stephen Tumim, the Chief Inspector of Prisons, condemns the regime at the Wolds prison. Complaints include 'corrupting lethargy', high incidence of violence and drug abuse

September '93. Norman Fowler resigns from board of G4. J. Philip-Sorensen said, 'Norman has been a personal friend for over 30 years and I have valued his wise counsel over the years'.

November '93. G4 acquires remaining 50% share in eco-friendly detergent, Ecover, becoming sole shareholder of the company. Darrell Barson found dead in his cell at the Wolds, hanging by his shoelaces. Later inquest rules suicide. Barson was on 15-minute suicide watch, but had not been seen for several hours before his death. The prison doctor said staff were too inexperienced to tell suicidal behaviour from signs of drug abuse, and that 90% of the prisoners he saw were 'drugged up to the eyeballs'.

September '94. G4 agrees not to use excessive force at the Stanworth Valley protest camp after an injunction application made by Chris Maile, and son Philip, of local Green Party.

October '94. Philip Maile hospitalised after G4 security guard illegally used pressure point hold to the back of his head – spent three weeks in neck collar.

May '95. Following consultation with Home Office, G4 to set up UK's first 'private riot squads' to deal with future disorder at immigration detention centres. Harbhajan Birdi accuses G4 of racism after his job application was rejected. He resubmitted an identical application changing his name and nationality to John Smith, British, and was short-listed for interview. Industrial tribunal later upholds racial discrimination. G4 agrees out-of-court settlement

February '96. Two G4 employees charged with looting a warehouse guarded by G4.

August '96. G4 won £14m contract to inspect up to 2000 nursery schools. The NUT and teachers groups sceptical about G4's suitability

Mar '98. Serious riot at Port Philip prison, Melbourne, initially described by G4 management as a 'passive demonstration'. Opened in August '97, Port Philip has been blighted by drug abuse, violence, and suicides. 60 staff resigned in the first 7 months.

www.corporatewatch.org.uk

'hypnotism, telepathy & occultism'. Methodist–Presbyterian schisms and the Liverpool crusade of Evan Roberts. 1913 saw the publication of 'War on the Saints', a controversial tract Evan Roberts co-authored (though he later disowned it) with Jessie Penn-Lewis, at whose home Roberts had convalesced after suffering a breakdown in 1906. Roberts' withdrawal from public life was in stark contrast to his prominence within the Revivalist movement. The charismatic 26-year-old former coalminer was still in study for his ministry when he found himself at the forefront of a massive upsurge in congregational activity throughout Wales. The Evangelical fervour spread to Liverpool at word of Roberts' plan to visit the city, prior to which he spent a week at Neath in total silence, and on a visit to his birthplace, Loughor, he gave away all of the money he owned.

The Liverpool crusade took in a number of Nonconformist chapels of varying persuasion. Roberts' sermons drew huge crowds, with most reportedly having to gather outside the already packed venues (Sun Hall in Kensington accommodated an attendance in the region of 6,000). At this juncture the city's numerous Presbyterian congregations were at odds, with many adherents abandoning their chapels to form new ones. Subsequent feelings of resentment and rivalry were in evidence at Roberts' orations and were exacerbated by the minister's confrontational and intransigent tone. In one meeting he called for the chapel to be cleansed as there were persons present who could not forgive each other. At another he claimed that the Holy Spirit had left the congregation as orphans as five notable worshippers could be identified, three being ministers, who were jealous of his successful works. The proceedings at Sun Hall were continuously disrupted, at one stage by an alleged attempt to hypnotise Roberts from within the crowd (the following day Dr Walford Bodie, the celebrated concert hall magician, admitted to being behind the stunt).

As the campaign continued, dogged by controversy, Roberts' opponents lined up in the local press to denounce him. One such adversary, the Reverend Daniel Hughes of Chester, wrote to *The Liverpool Courier*:

Sir – Evan Roberts is no psychological problem to me. I claim to understand what arts he uses to produce the desired effects, and, what his secret is. His silence is essential to his success, his interruptions have a purpose, his prophetic utterances are perfectly sane. I

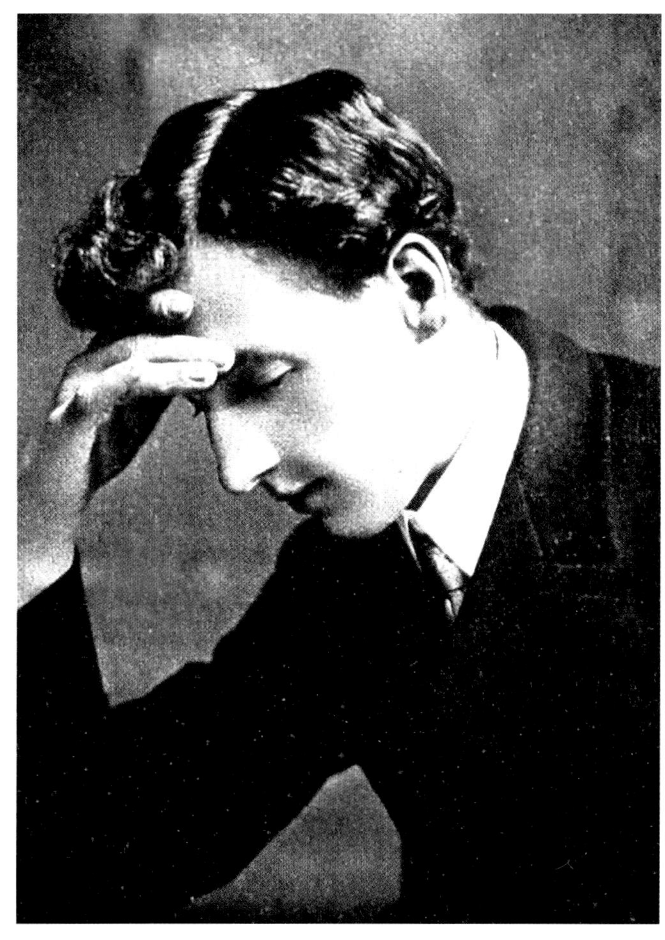

hope to follow this young genius (for genius he is) through the country to deliver a lecture in English and Welsh entitled: "Evan Roberts explained and exposed". That he should do this in the name of the Holy Spirit is blasphemy.
Yours &c. (Rev) Daniel Hughes. April 14th 1905

As his work in Liverpool drew to a close, Roberts began to show symptoms of the ill health that would shadow him for the rest of his days. Another of his critics, the Reverend H.M. Roberts, had at a final gathering on 17 April gone back on his condemnations, and now claimed that *'Evan Roberts was the nearest human being to Jesus, and resembled him more than any other religious leader'*.

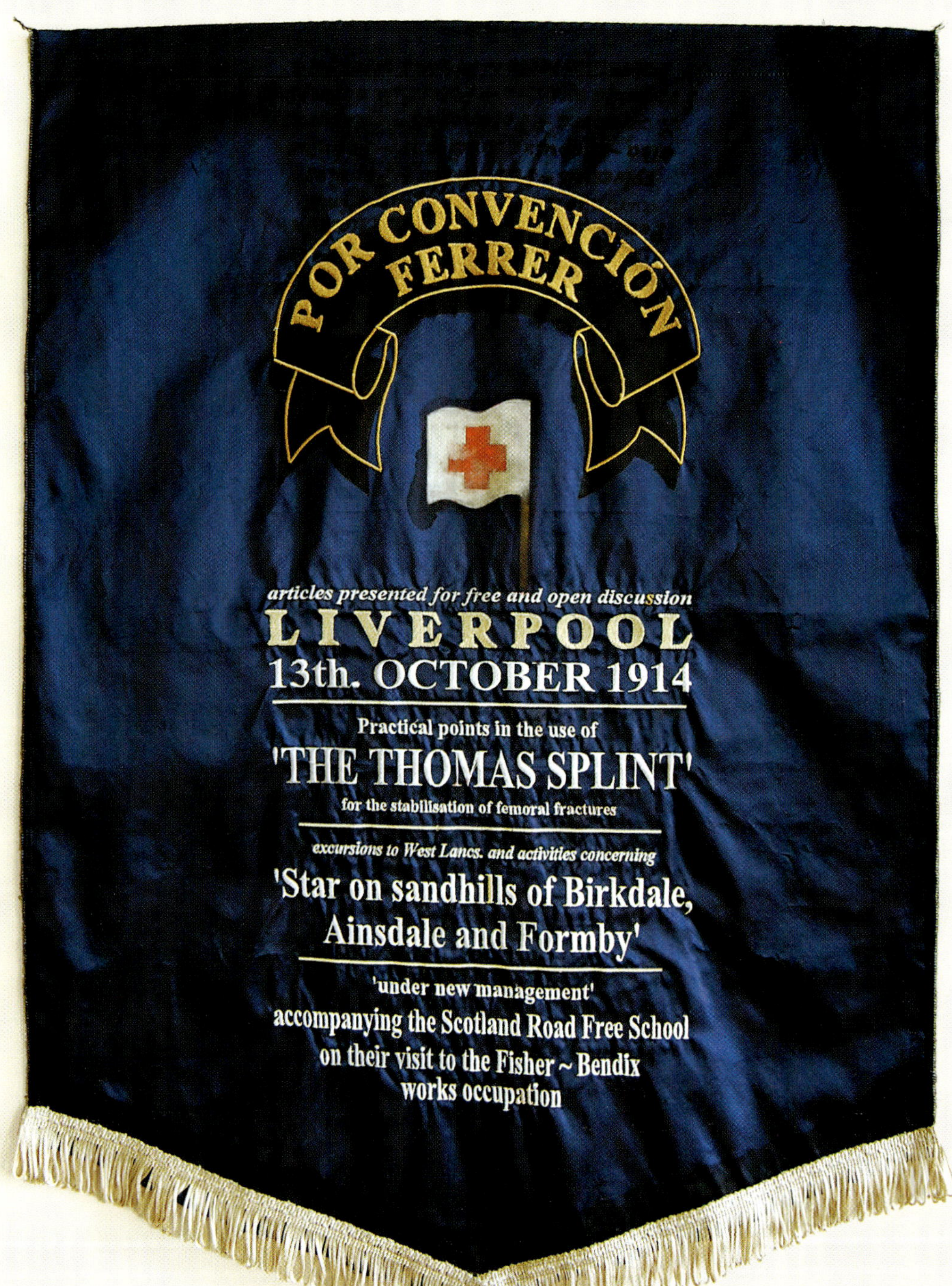
POR CONVENCIÓN
FERRER
articles presented for free and open discussion
LIVERPOOL
13th. OCTOBER 1914
Practical points in the use of
'THE THOMAS SPLINT'
for the stabilisation of femoral fractures
excursions to West Lancs. and activities concerning
'Star on sandhills of Birkdale,
Ainsdale and Formby'
'under new management'
accompanying the Scotland Road Free School
on their visit to the Fisher ~ Bendix
works occupation

In 1914 the conference saw a practical demonstration of the 'Thomas Splint', had an account of a visit to the sand dunes at Thomas Weld-Blundell's estate and made a tour of the worker-occupied Fisher-Bendix factory in Kirkby.

Por Convención Ferrer

LIVERPOOL

13 October 1914

Concerning practical points in the use of
'The Thomas Splint'
for the stabilisation of femoral fractures

Excursions to West Lancs and activities concerning
'Star on Sandhills of Birkdale, Ainsdale and Formby'

'under new management'
**accompanying the Scotland Road Free School
during their visit to the Fisher-Bendix
works occupation**

Concerning practical points in the use of 'The Thomas Splint' for the stabilisation of femoral fractures. Though by and large overlooked by the medical establishment during his lifetime, Hugh Owen Thomas is generally considered to have been a pioneering figure in the history of orthopaedic surgery. He came from the island of Anglesey off the North Wales coast, where his family had assumed the unqualified profession of 'bone-setting', a practice which, in the wake of his medical studies in London, Thomas was to distance himself from. Most of his professional life was spent in the run-down districts of Liverpool treating the poor, among whom by all accounts he was held in high regard.

His ideas and innovations were published in *Diseases of the hip, knee and ankle joints, with their deformities treated by a new and efficient method* (T. Dobb & Co., Liverpool, 1875). With regards to the treatment of tuberculosis and fractures, he strongly advocated the use of rest, which should be *'enforced, uninterrupted and prolonged'.* This was contrary to the received wisdom of the day, which more often recommended excision or amputation for chronic bone disorders. His contribution to the management of fractures was not widely recognised until after his death, and in particular after the onset of the First World War, where the introduction of the 'Thomas splint' (supervised by his nephew, the Inspector of Military Orthopaedics Robert Jones) contributed to the mortality rate of compound fractures of the femur falling from 80 per cent in 1916 to less than 8 per cent in 1918.

Excursions to West Lancs and activities concerning 'Star on Sandhills of Birkdale, Ainsdale and Formby'. From as early as the mid-1700s an Act of Parliament had endorsed a sometime manorial duty on tenants to plant marram ('Star' or 'Bent') grass on the landowners' estate. The planting of marram, as overseen by 'Star lookers', ensured the stabilisation of sand dunes (and by extension the viability of land for sale or appropriation), but the grass was also an ideal material for the making of woven domestic ware such as thatch, floor mats or brushes.

On 15 August 1857 a notice was served by the attorney for the Weld–Blundell family warning against the taking of marram grass from their estate:

'WHEREAS, frequent notices have heretofore been given, that it is unlawful for any person to cut, pull up, or carry away any Star on or from the Hills of Birkdale, Ainsdale, and Formby; or for any person to have any Star in his or her custody or possession, or to trespass on the said Hills. Painted boards have also been put up in these Townships, warning persons against these acts, but several of these boards have been maliciously destroyed. Notwithstanding these repeated Notices, they have been found insufficient to deter persons from trespassing on the said Sandhills, and from cutting, pulling up, and carrying away Star, and from having the same in their possession, and such offences having greatly increased.'

NOTICE IS HEREBY GIVEN

'THAT by act of parliament, 15 Geo. II., Cap. 33, if any person shall, without the consent of the Lord or owner, cut, pull up, or carry away any Star or Bent, planted or set on the sandhills, it is made lawful for any Justice, on complaint on oath, to summon the Offender, and in default of appearance thereon, to issue out his warrant to apprehend and bring before him such Offender; and of proof thereof made, to convict him of twenty shillings, to be levied by distress and sale of the Offenders' Goods, and for want of sufficient distress, to commit the Offender to the House of Correction for Three Months, to be kept to hard labour. AND for a Second Offence, he shall be committed to the House of Correction for One Year, and to be Whipped and kept to hard labour.

'under new management'. Accompanying the Scotland Road Free School during their visit to the Fisher-Bendix works occupation. The Scotland Road Free School operated out of the Vauxhall Community Services Centre, Silvester Street, Liverpool for approximately two years in the early 70s. From a leaflet posted around homes in the Vauxhall ward, summer 1971:

'There will be set up in the Scotland Road – Vauxhall area of Liverpool, an alternative type of school to be known as the Scotland Road Free School. The school will be a community school which will be totally involved with its environment. The nature of this involvement will be such that the school will be in the vanguard of social change in the area. By accepting this role, the school will not seek to impose its own values, but will have as its premise a total acceptance of the people and the area …

The ultimate aim of the free school is to bring about a fragmentation of the state system into smaller, all age, personalized, democratic, locally controlled community schools which can best serve the immediate needs of the area in which they are situated. It is felt that the state system in contemplating change considers only innocuous reforms which do not question the full structure. We are obliged therefore to step outside the system in order to best demonstrate the feasibility and fulfillment of the free school ideal. Having achieved this demonstration we are sure that society will enforce the adoption of the free school idea by the state system …

The school will not have a headmaster or hierarchy, nor will it recognize any central authority, but will be controlled by the parents, children and teachers together. This would be achieved democratically through a school council. The school will operate as a day school but will never close whilst people desire to use its facilities. Lessons will not be compulsory, the onus will be on the teacher to stimulate the children sufficiently to attend. At the same time the school will offer its participants a range of social and academic activities comparable with state schools. These activities will be ascertained by observation and pupil–staff consultation …'

One memorable field trip undertaken by the school involved a visit to the Fisher-Bendix works occupation on the Kirkby Industrial Estate. The slogan **'under new management'** was pasted over the company sign at the factory gates during the dispute.

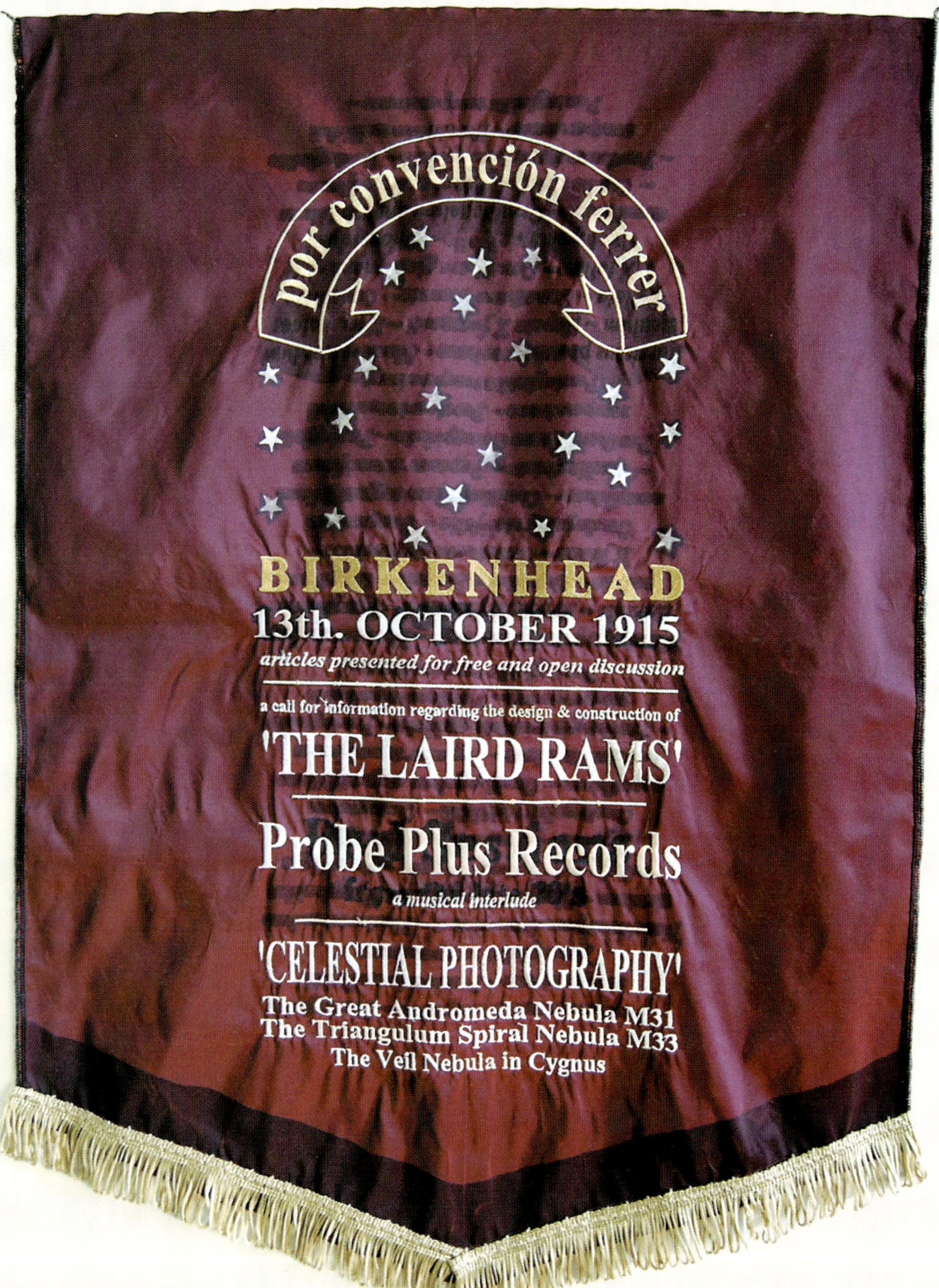

por convención ferrer
BIRKENHEAD
13th. OCTOBER 1915
articles presented for free and open discussion
a call for information regarding the design & construction of
'THE LAIRD RAMS'
Probe Plus Records
a musical interlude
'CELESTIAL PHOTOGRAPHY'
The Great Andromeda Nebula M31
The Triangulum Spiral Nebula M33
The Veil Nebula in Cygnus

The conference in Birkenhead ran with a call for assistance forwarded from the office of Thomas Haines Dudley, a musical interlude comprised of 'demo tapes', followed by an astro-photographic projection show.

Por Convención Ferrer

BIRKENHEAD

13 October 1915

A call for information regarding the design & construction of
'The Laird Rams'

Probe Plus Records
A musical interlude

'Celestial Photography'
The Great Andromeda NebulaM31
The Triangulum Spiral Nebula M33
The Veil Nebula in Cygnus

A call for information regarding the design & construction of 'The Laird Rams' was relayed to the conference. The diplomatic engagements between the Confederacy, the Union and the British Palmerston Government are often cited as a determining factor in the outcome of the American Civil War. These engagements were shadowed by a widespread and elaborate use of covert activity, through intelligence gathering, espionage and counter-espionage. As a strategically important seaport, Liverpool became a focal point for such pursuits. Thomas Haines Dudley, a lawyer from New Jersey, set up office in the city as consul for the US and began a long war of attrition against Confederate covert operations.

'I had hoped that ... the prospect of a speedy termination of the rebellion would have the effect to discourage the friends and allies of the rebels in this country & prevent the fitting out of vessels and expeditions to aid them in the unholy work of trying to destroy the government. But contrary to my hopes and expectations it seems not to have any effect on them. The business goes on as actively as at any previous period.' T.H. Dudley to US Secretary of State, William H. Seward, 21 May 1862

The Confederate naval officer James Dunwoody Bulloch arrived in Liverpool unofficially with orders to commission the construction, albeit illegally, of warships to advance the South's naval powers. Two such warships were ordered in 1862 from the Laird shipyard and became known as 'The Laird Rams'. Steam-powered and ironclad, each would possess an array of armament and firepower as well as an underwater ram capable of sinking any wooden-hulled vessel.

On completion of both ships, information obtained by Dudley asserting Confederate ownership was used in evidence to detain and decommission the vessels, a significant victory which led to the dissolution in British shipyards of a modern Confederate Navy.

Probe Plus Records. A musical interlude. Geoff Davies interviewed by Gary Logan, 20 August 1992.

Do you still get inundated with demo tapes?

Yeah, I still get tapes sent – I'm just not in a position to do anything with them. It's just so bad at the moment. Over the last year I've been completely on my arse, not taking a wage out or anything. It's been as bad as it can get.

But it's a labour of love for you really. Do you like most of the bands on your label?

Practically all.

Would you take on a band if you thought that they would make you lots of money, even if you hated their music or them?

No, probably not. I can't work with people that I find to be arseholes.

So if Michael Jackson came to you and offered his services?

(Laughs) No he'd get on my fucking nerves would Michael. I turned down Frankie goes to Hollywood for instance. Paul Rutherford used to work in the shop and he said 'I've got a tape of the band, and you'll hate it, but listen to it …' I did hate it! Pete Burns of Dead or Alive who used to work for me is a good lad and a mate and all that, but he would be such a pain in the arse and so petulant. I knew him too well, I couldn't work for him. I can't be dealing with ego sort of bands, or do a record for bands that just want to make it out of Liverpool and that applies to so many Liverpool bands. I've done a lot of things that I think have an edge to them, something different. There are about 500 bands playing in Liverpool and most of them are complete and utter dreck. Poppy, mid-Atlantic, with no reflection of the lives of these people …

'Celestial Photography'. The Great Andromeda Nebula M31, The Triangulum Spiral Nebula M33, The Veil Nebula in Cygnus. 'Celestial Photography' was the title of an influential pamphlet on astro-photography, published through the Liverpool Astronomical Society in 1914. The images of 'The Great Andromeda Nebula', 'The Triangulum Nebula' and 'The Veil Nebula in Cygnus' featured in 'A Selection of Photographs of Stars, Star-clusters and Nebulae' (Vol. I 1893 & Vol. II 1899) were the work of the self-taught astronomer Isaac Roberts (1829–1904).

Roberts' pioneering studies began whilst living in Rock Ferry on the Wirral Peninsula. The difficulties Victorian astronomers encountered in picturing deep space objects were solved by the telescope, camera and tracking device combination he developed. This facilitated the long exposures required to render clear and detailed imagery, which entailed Roberts being the first person to identify the spiral shape of the Great Andromeda Nebula, showing it to be the same type of object as the spiral nebulae. He found that the Pleiades star cluster contained extensive nebulosity between the stars and discovered the Great Orion Nebula to be much larger and structurally complex than previously thought.

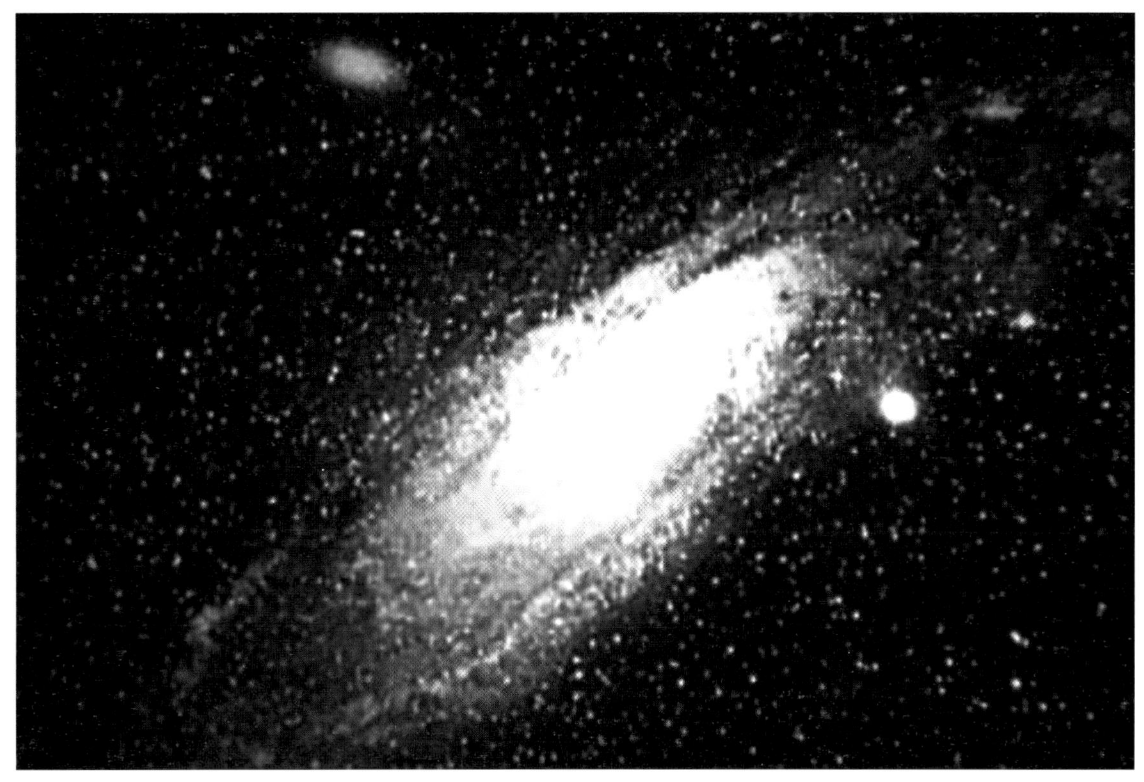

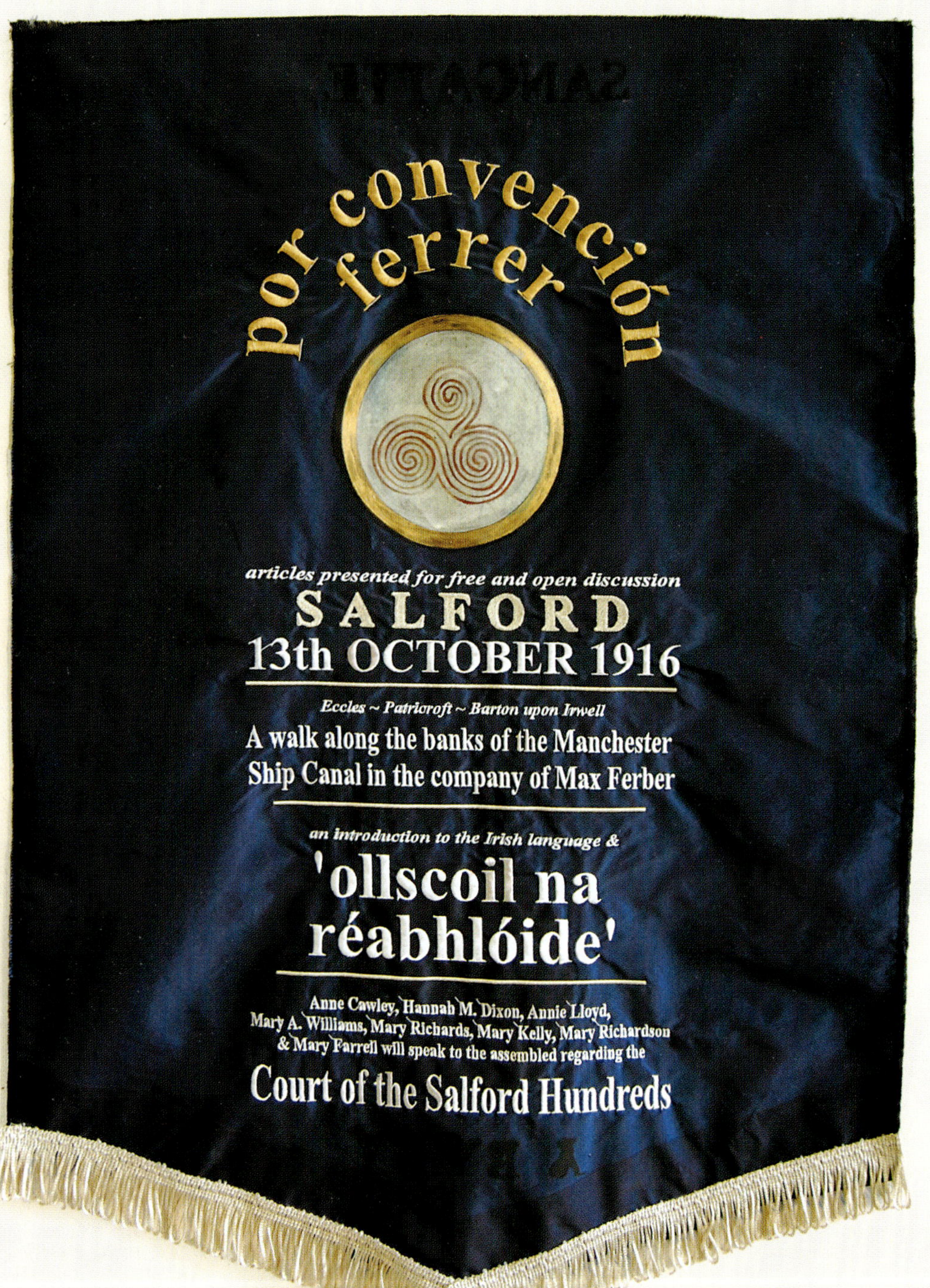
por convención ferrer
articles presented for free and open discussion
SALFORD
13th OCTOBER 1916
Eccles ~ Patricroft ~ Barton upon Irwell
A walk along the banks of the Manchester Ship Canal in the company of Max Ferber
an introduction to the Irish language &
'ollscoil na réabhlóide'
Anne Cawley, Hannah M. Dixon, Annie Lloyd, Mary A. Williams, Mary Richards, Mary Kelly, Mary Richardson & Mary Farrell will speak to the assembled regarding the
Court of the Salford Hundreds

The conference of 1916 involved a walk along the Manchester Ship Canal, a talk by a fugitive Irish Republican and a discussion held outside the Court of the Salford Hundreds.

Por Convención Ferrer

SALFORD

13 October 1916

Eccles – Patricroft – Barton upon Irwell
A walk along the banks of the Manchester Ship Canal in the company of Max Ferber

An introduction to the Irish language &
'ollscoil na réabhlóide'

Anne Cawley, Hannah M. Dixon, Annie Lloyd, Mary A. Williams, Mary Richards, Mary Kelly, Mary Richardson & Mary Farrell will speak to the assembled regarding the
Court of the Salford Hundreds

Eccles – Patricroft – Barton upon Irwell. A walk along the banks of the Manchester Ship Canal in the company of Max Ferber.

Max Ferber is a fictitious character, a Jewish émigré and artist, from *The Emigrants* by W.G. Sebald published in 1996 (Harvill Press)

'One summer evening in 1966, nine or ten months after my arrival in Manchester, Ferber and I were walking along the Ship Canal embankment, past the suburbs of Eccles, Patricroft and Barton upon Irwell on the other side of the black water, towards the setting sun and the scattered outskirts where occasional views opened up, affording an intimation of the marshes that extended there as late as the mid-nineteenth century. The Manchester Ship Canal, Ferber told me, was begun in 1887 and completed in 1894. The work was mainly done by a continuously reinforced army of Irish navvies, who shifted some sixty million cubic metres of earth in that period and built the gigantic locks that would make it possible to raise or lower ocean-going steamers up to 150 metres long by five or six metres. Manchester was then the industrial Jerusalem, said Ferber, its entrepreneurial spirit and progressive vigour the envy of the world, and the completion of the immense canal project had made it the largest inland port on earth. Ships of the Canada & Newfoundland Steamship Company, the China Mutual Line, the Manchester Bombay General Navigation Company, and many other shipping lines, plied the docks near the city centre. The loading and unloading never stopped: wheat, nitre, construction timber, cotton, rubber, jute. train oil, tobacco, tea, coffee, cane sugar, exotic fruits, copper and iron ore, steel, machinery, marble and mahogany – everything, in fact that could possibly be needed, processed or made in a manufacturing metropolis of that order. Manchester's shipping traffic peaked around 1930 and then went into an irreversible decline, till it came to a complete standstill in the late Fifties. Given the motionlessness and deathly silence that lay upon the canal now, it was difficult to imagine, said Ferber, as we gazed back at the city sinking into the twilight, that he himself, in the postwar years, had seen the most enormous freighters on this water. They would slip slowly by, and as they approached the port they passed amidst houses, looming high above the black slate roofs. And in winter, said Ferber, if a ship suddenly appeared out of the mist when one least expected it, passed by soundlessly, and vanished once more in the white air, then for me, every time, it was an utterly incomprehensible spectacle which moved me deeply.'

An introduction to the Irish language & 'ollscoil na réabhlóide' (The 'University of Revolution'). In the wake of the 1916 uprising in Dublin, almost 2,000 captured Republicans were transported to an internment camp at Frongoch, North Wales. The decision to amass in one place a hard-core though previously disparate grouping inadvertently played into the Republicans' hands.

'Had the British Government known what was taking place under their very own guard and officials, we would have been hunted out of the camp, for it must be realized that men came together in that camp from all parts of Ireland; from towns, villages and places that would have taken years to bring together for the work which had to be done, especially in the training of the army of the Republic.' Thomas Leahy, witness statement to the Irish Bureau of Military History

As well as militaristic training, the internees at Frongoch initiated an educational programme that flourished during the lifespan of the camp. Classes in subjects such as Irish language, history, mathematics, book-keeping and telegraphing were provided and maintained by volunteers who had, in the main, originated from the teaching professions.

Anne Cawley, Hannah M. Dixon, Annie Lloyd, Mary A. Williams, Mary Richards, Mary Kelly, Mary Richardson & Mary Farrell will speak to the assembled regarding the Court of the Salford Hundreds. These eight names were the known aliases used by Mary Davies when prosecuted for petty theft between 1886 and 1890. Salford Hundred Court sat for the trial of civil actions every three weeks on debt or damage under 40/-. It was amalgamated with the Manchester Court of Record in 1868.

A random selection of cases tried at the Salford Hundreds, 2 March 1867; taking previous convictions into account explains inconsistencies in sentencing:

NAME	AGE	PROFESSION	OFFENCE	SENTENCE
Thomas Tweedale	30	factory operator	stealing shawl	7 years
Ashton Wroe	32	labourer	embezzling £1.3s.6d	3 months
Ann Johnson	44	charwoman	stealing from clothes line	2 months
William Stannard	22	sweep	stealing half-crown	7 years
Ann Donavan	26	hawker	stealing 2 blankets & 1 sheet	4 months
John Fletcher	29	bricklayer	stealing 57 yards of wincey	7 years
Henry Bleckly	20	dyer	stealing 8 hens & 1 cock	3 months
Mary Power	15	servant	stealing clothes	18 months

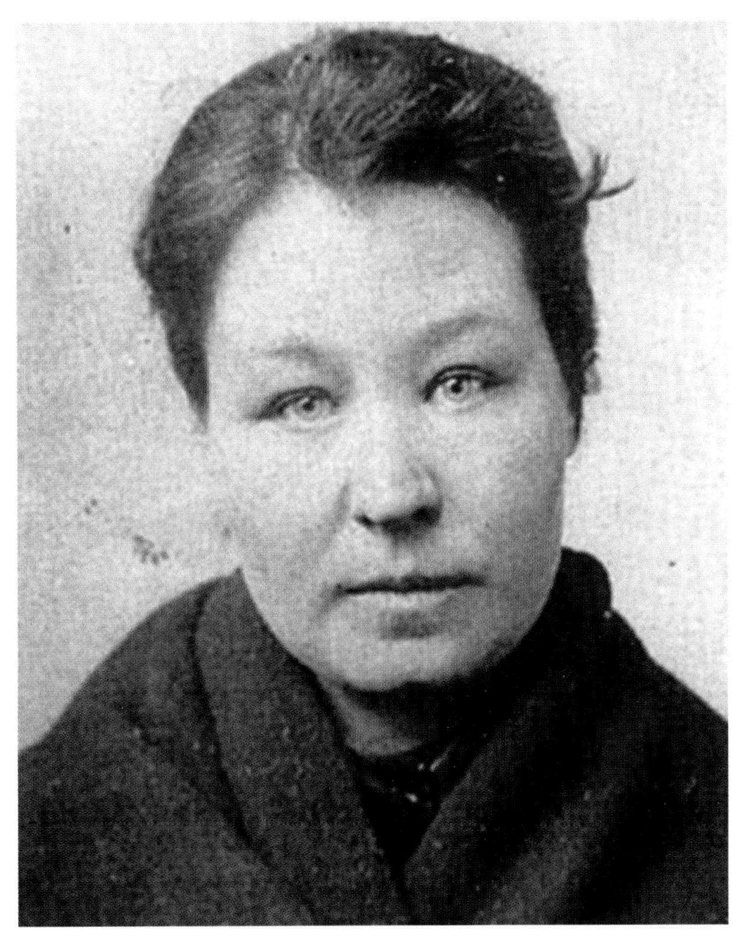

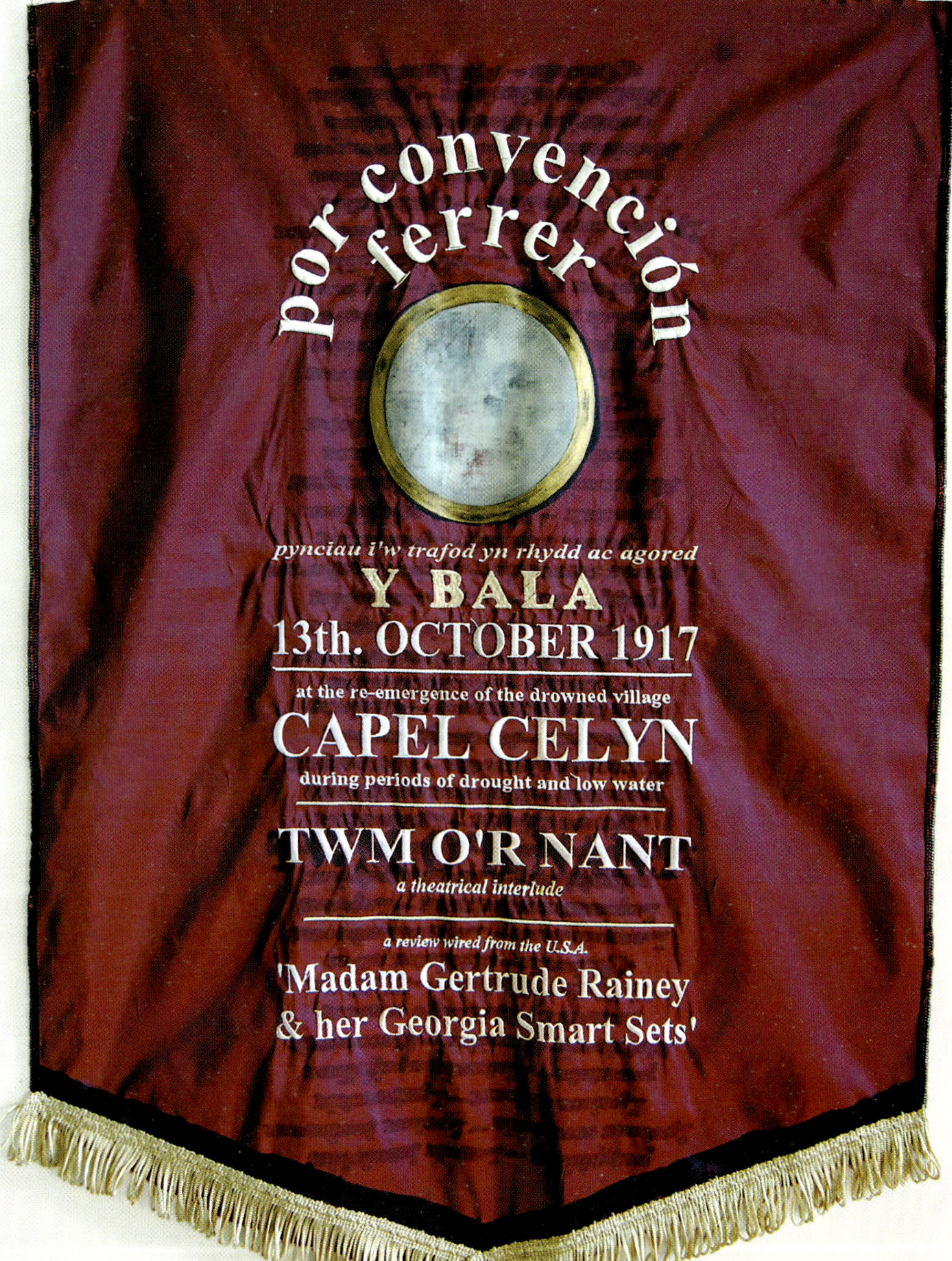

por convención
ferrer
pynciau i'w trafod yn rhydd ac agored
Y BALA
13th. OCTOBER 1917
at the re-emergence of the drowned village
CAPEL CELYN
during periods of drought and low water
TWM O'R NANT
a theatrical interlude
a review wired from the U.S.A.
'Madam Gertrude Rainey
& her Georgia Smart Sets'

The Bala conference entailed a visit to the reservoir at Tryweryn, a review of Gertrude 'Ma' Rainey's 1917 tour of the US Southern States and a theatrical performance overseen by the bard Twm o'r Nant.

Por Convención Ferrer

Y BALA

13 October 1917

at the re-emergence of the drowned village
Capel Celyn
during periods of drought and low water

Twm o'r Nant
A theatrical interlude

a review wired from the USA
'Madam Gertrude Rainey
& her Georgia Smart Sets'

at the re-emergence of the drowned village Capel Celyn during periods of drought and low water.

'Glittering cities, say the fables, lie beneath Welsh waters, bells are heard hauntingly from the deep, towers are glimpsed by fishermen far down among the waterweeds. There can be substance to the fancy. The remains of a prehistoric stilted village at Llyn Syfaddan give a frail confirmation to one of Defoe's rejected legends, and now and then our own times have ironically turned tradition into prophecy; for in several parts of Wales modern reservoirs have drowned entire communities, and when their water levels are low sometimes you really can see the rotting shells of houses and chapels jutting from the mud …

'In the 1950s the Corporation of Liverpool, in England, decided that the valley of the small river Tryweryn, running down to the Dee near Y Bala, would make a convenient reservoir for the supply of free water to Merseyside. The fact that the hamlet of Capel Celyn stood in the middle of the site did not deter them; nor did the fact that it was one of the very Welshest parts of all Wales. Their brochure describing the project did not mention that it was in Wales at all, and the name of not a single Welshman appeared upon it; the water engineer was from Liverpool, the consulting engineers were from London, the landscape consultant was Frederick Gibberd, CBE, the contractors were from Wolverhampton and the Fishery Advisor from Aberdeen. The Welsh local authorities found themselves powerless to oppose the scheme, and Welsh patriots were infuriated by it – nearly thirty years later the slogan 'COFIWCH DRYWERYN' 'Remember Tryweryn', is still to be seen in fading white paint on rocks and stone walls here and there; but it made no difference anyway …' Jan Morris, *Wales – epic views of a small country* (Penguin, 1986)

Twm o'r Nant. A theatrical interlude. Presented by his travelling band of performers. According to his autobiography (published 1849), Twm o'r Nant was born Thomas Edwards in January 1738 in the parish of Llannefydd, Denbighshire. Largely self-taught (his schooling was scant and solely in the English language), for the most part he worked as a timber haulier, though early in his career his fortunes suffered a major downturn when he lost his horses to disease and an uncle he stood surety for fell bankrupt, leaving him with insurmountable debts. Twm's only option at this point was to hightail it out of town, eventually settling in Llandeilo where once again he became a haulier.

The way was cleared for Twm's return to Denbighshire when he was able to address his financial problems with money earned through the writing of 'interludes', short stories generally produced for performance, which Twm often acted in himself. The satirical nature of his work revealed Twm's antipathy towards authority. His targets ranged from the Church, which he saw as immoral, aloof (often pointing to a common inability to communicate in Welsh) and lacking in spiritual guidance for its flock, through to absentee, profiteering landowners and tax collectors.

Though he undoubtedly found favour with the many who came to watch his travelling band, his submissions to competition at successive eisteddfods went unrewarded. Most notably so at Corwen in 1789, when at being controversially overlooked for a prize he found an ally in Captain Cook's surgeon, David Samwel. Samwel gave Twm a silver writing pen for his efforts, but also stuck him with the unfortunately overblown title of the 'Cambrian Shakespeare'.

A review wired from the USA. 'Madam Gertrude Rainey & her Georgia Smart Sets'. Madam Gertrude Rainey, or 'Ma' Rainey, embarked on an extensive tour in 1917 after separating from her husband, the musician William 'Pa' Rainey. As her career developed, her reputation for flamboyant and sexually transgressive behaviour blossomed, along with her particular influence on the burgeoning blues music scene. Song titles in her set at this point included 'Memphis Blues', Jelly Roll Blues' and 'See see rider'.

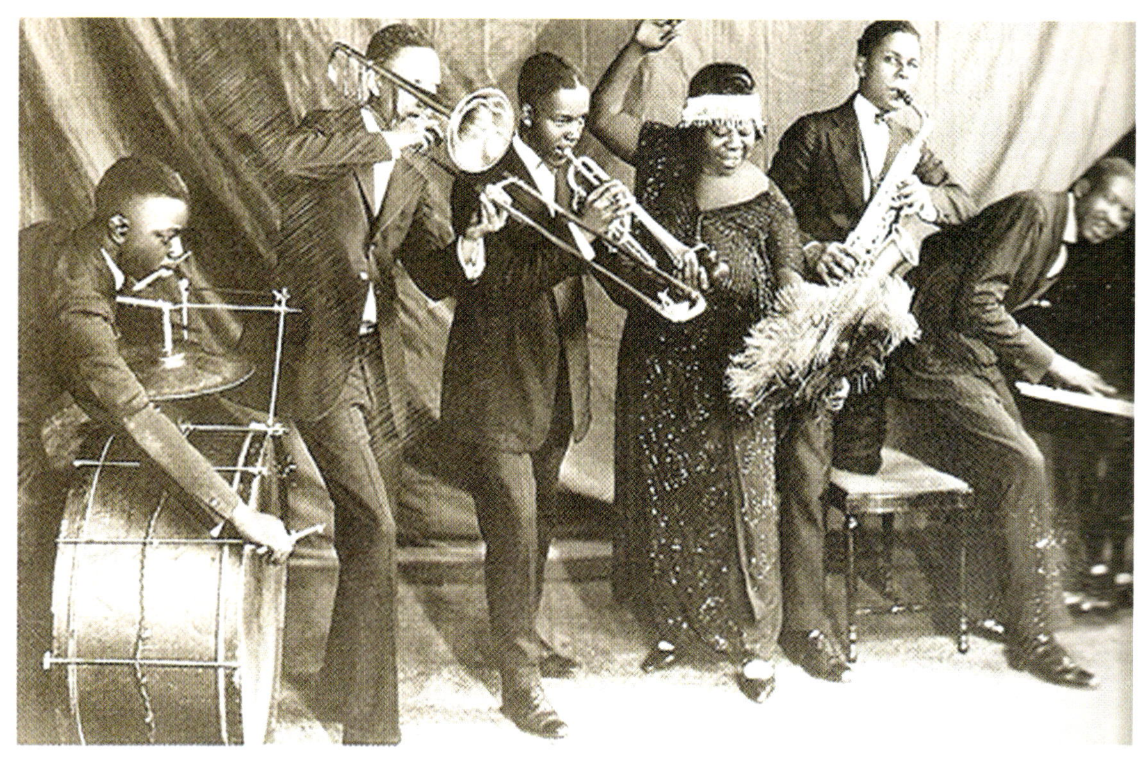

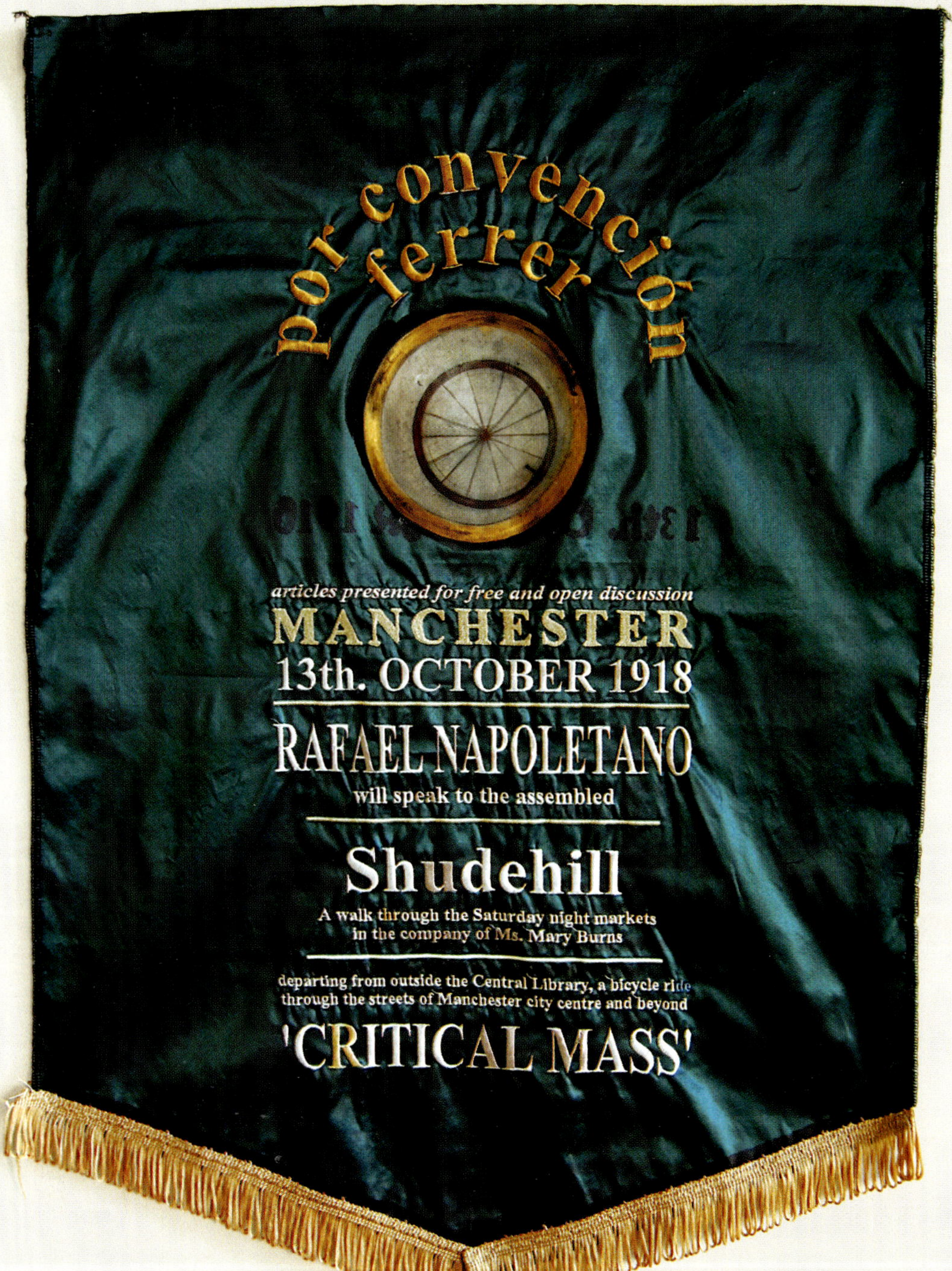
por convención ferrer
articles presented for free and open discussion
MANCHESTER
13th. OCTOBER 1918
RAFAEL NAPOLETANO
will speak to the assembled
Shudehill
A walk through the Saturday night markets
in the company of Ms. Mary Burns
departing from outside the Central Library, a bicycle ride
through the streets of Manchester city centre and beyond
'CRITICAL MASS'

The final outing included a talk given by an ex-serviceman from the 1st Manchester Regt., a walk through the Saturday night markets at Shudehill and an invitation to join a 'Critical Mass' bike ride.

Por Convención Ferrer

MANCHESTER

13 October 1918

Rafael Napoletano
will speak to the assembled

Shudehill
A walk through the Saturday night markets
in the company of Ms. Mary Burns

departing from outside the Central Library, a bicycle ride
through the streets of Manchester City Centre and beyond
'Critical Mass'

Rafael Napoletano will speak to the assembled. From a series of correspondences between the Town Clerk, Cardiff City Hall and the Town Clerk, Municipal Buildings Liverpool, dated 26 September 1919:

Dear Sir,
Rafael Napoletano
I desire to revert to previous correspondence with reference to the case of this Alien lunatic, and in particular to the second paragraph of your letter of the 2nd July last. I fear you have been misinformed as to the time and place where the man became of unsound mind.

Particulars furnished to me by the clerk to the Cardiff Guardians were as follows: Napoletano joined the British Army in America and was afterwards attached to the 1st. Manchester Regt. He was admitted to Crookslon Mental Hospital, Neathshill near Glasgow from which Institution he escaped and was found wandering at Liverpool, where a deportation order was made for him to be sent to Italy.

It is quite clear from the foregoing that the Alien had been certified as a lunatic, and the fact that one of our Police surgeons issued a similar certificate whilst the lunatic was in the custody of the Cardiff Police by mutual arrangement and with the object of assisting your Police Authority in finding a boat on which the lunatic could be deported, does not make the lunatic chargeable to my authority. Liverpool and not Cardiff was the place where the lunatic was found wandering, and it is unreasonable and illogical to conclude that because the Cardiff Police engaged to assist your Police in the discharge of their official functions, my authority are to be saddled with an expenditure such as that involved in this case. It is true that the sum is not large but the principle involved is an important one. It cannot be contended that the actions of the Liverpool Police in bringing lunatics to this city and leaving them in charge of the Cardiff Police to deport them justifies either in a legal or moral sense the transfer of the financial obligations of the former to the latter.

In view of the foregoing facts, I trust your Authority will accept the responsibility for the maintenance of the lunatic during the period of his residence in the Newport Borough Asylum at Caerleon, and I shall be glad to hear from you that they will.

Yours faithfully
J. L. Wheatley
Town Clerk

Shudehill. A walk through the Saturday night markets in the company of Ms. Mary Burns. The Saturday night markets of Manchester and Salford from the 1840s onwards offered working-class people a source of cheap food and free entertainment.

'... alive with animation and amid a blaze of gas all is life and bustle. In the outskirts of the market place you may have yourself accurately weighed and measured for one halfpenny. For the same sum you may receive a shock from a galvanic battery. You may then enjoy a few minutes sporting, by shooting at a target over a rifle range extending about two yards ... you have thrown in free of charge, an oral lecture ... explanatory of a great portion of your own interior, accompanied, at a short distance, by the strains of an energetic Scotch fiddler requesting you to "come through the heather, around him gather, for wha'll be King but Charlie," and other patriotic and national sentiments'. Anon, 'A ramble through Shudehill Market', *Free Lance* (periodical), Vol. 2, No. 53, 1867

The daughter of Irish emigrants, Mary Burns lived in the impoverished district of Deansgate and was an active member of the Chartist movement. She was the partner of Friedrich Engels, with whom she lived until her death in 1862.

departing from outside the Central Library, a bicycle ride through the streets of Manchester City Centre and beyond. 'Critical Mass'. *'Critical Mass is often described as an "unorganised coincidence". It happens when a lot of cyclists happen to be in the same place at the same time and decide to cycle the same way together for a while. Everyday, all over the world, people are resisting the problem culture of the car by getting on their bikes and riding, instead of driving.*

Critical Mass is a celebration of the alternatives to cars; pollution, accidents and the loss of public spaces and freedoms. Not an organisation or group, but an idea or tactic, Critical Mass allows people to reclaim cities with their bikes, just by getting together and out-numbering the cars on the road. Each one is different and they follow no set route, with the direction being spontaneously chosen as people cycle along. Anyone is free to join or leave the ride as it pedals along.' Posted on numerous Critical Mass websites worldwide, 2007

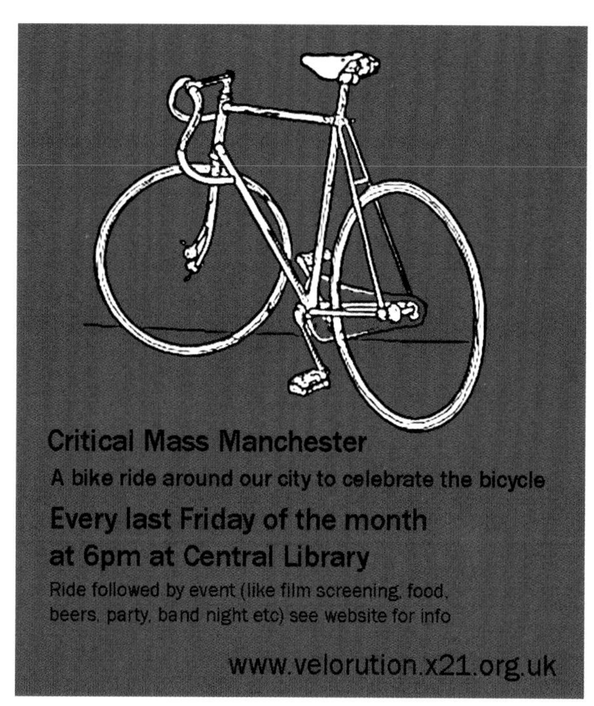
Critical Mass Manchester
A bike ride around our city to celebrate the bicycle
Every last Friday of the month
at 6pm at Central Library
Ride followed by event (like film screening, food,
beers, party, band night etc) see website for info
www.velorution.x21.org.uk

Selected further reading

Andrada, Martin and Spira, 'Inner Worlds Outside', Fundación la Caixa, I.M.M.A. and The Whitechapel Gallery, 2006.

Atkinson, D. and Houston, J.A., *The Sand Dunes of the Sefton Coast*, National Nuseums and Galleries on Merseysde, 1993

Beynon, Huw, *Working for Ford*, Penguin, 1973

De Quincey, Thomas, *Confessions of an English Opium-Eater*, *The London Magazine*, 1821

Ebenezer, Lyn, *Fron-goch & the birth of the I.R.A.*, Gwasg Carreg Gwalch, 2005

Finch, John Jr. & The Liverpool Anti-Monopoly Association, 'Statistics of Vauxhall Ward, Liverpool', J. Walmsley, London, 1842.

Holton, Bob, 'Syndicalism and Labour in Merseyside 1906–14', in *Building the Union*, Toulouse Press, 1973

Jones, Steve, *Manchester – the sinister side*, Wicked publications, 1997

Logan, Gary, 'Geoff Davies', *'Strangled'* fanzine, August 1992

Lyons, Maryinez, *The Colonial Disease – A social history of sleeping sickness in Zaire, 1900–1940*, Cambridge University Press, 1992

Milton, David Hepburn, *Lincoln's Spymaster – Thomas Haines Dudley & the Liverpool Network*, Stackpole Books, 2003

Morris, Jan, *Wales – epic views of a small country*, Penguin, 1986

Rees, D. Ben, *The Welsh of Merseyside – volume 1*, Modern Welsh Publications Ltd

Roberts, Isaac, 'A Selection of Photographs of Stars, Star-clusters and Nebulae', Vol. I, 1893 & Vol. II, 1899

Sebald, W.G., *The Emigrants*, The Harvill Press 1996

Stevens, Albert C., *The Cyclopaedia of Fraternities*, Hamilton Printing and Publishing Co., New York, 1899

Thomas, Hugh Owen, *Diseases of the hip, knee and ankle joints, with their deformities treated by a new and efficient method*, T. Dobb & Co., Liverpool, 1875

Acknowledgments: Many thanks to James Brian Jacques, Suzanne Rudkin, Peter Naylor, Frank Boyce, Paul Farley, Marguerite O'Molloy & Georgie Thompson (Irish Museum of Modern Art), Monika Kinley (Musgrave Kinley Outsider Art Collection), Anne & Robin Hunt, Dr. D. Ben Rees (Merseyside Welsh Heritage Society), Joe Farrag, Alan Dunn, The Family Refugee Support Project Liverpool, Steve Higginson, Liz Molyneux and Ian, Jah, Kevin & Paul at Tabacula Films. With photography by Angela Mounsey and Craig Matthews.

Page 11. Michael the Cartographer, Untitled, Felt tip pen on paper, 20.8 x 30 cm
Collection Irish Museum of Modern Art, On loan from the Musgrave Kinley Outsider Art Collection
Photographer Denis Mortell

Page 49. Photograph of Mary Davies by kind permission of West Midlands Police Museum.

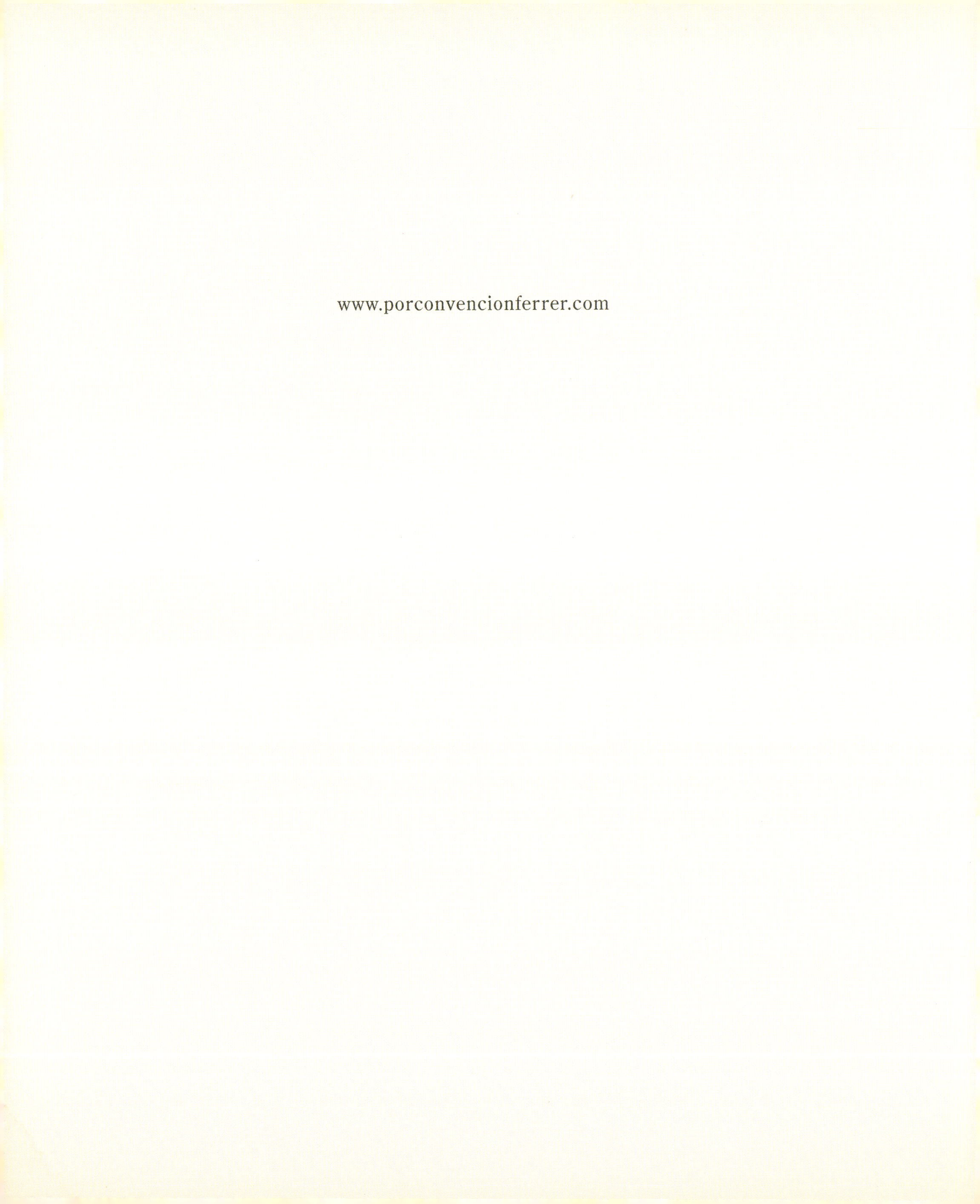
www.porconvencionferrer.com